When A Man
WORSHIPS

When A Man
WORSHIPS

Mark A. Williams, M.D., Ph.D.

All Things All People
PUBLISHING

ISBN: 978-0-9702377-8-1 (print)

ISBN: 978-0-9702377-9-8 (electronic)

Contact Copyright Holder at:

Mark A. Williams, M.D., Ph.D., All Things All People Publishing, P.O. Box 110793, Nashville, TN 37222, USA; Booking@atapmusic.com; +1 (615) 724-0131

Published non-exclusively by:

All Things All People Publishing, LLC, 8877 Meadowview Drive, Westchester, Ohio 45069

This book is dedicated to my parents, the late Charles and Mary Williams, for the strong foundation they laid and to my wife, Darice, and children (Demarcus, Aaron & Courtney) for the real-life education.

Contents

INTRODUCTION

G od created mankind to worship. However, there is
something unique about a man who has mastered
the essence of worship. Uncommon things happen *when
a man worships.* This does not discredit the impact of a
worshiping woman, but I believe that worship initiated
and offered by a man compels God in a special way.
When God formed the earth, his most prized creation
was man. The original intent was for man to have
continual fellowship with God. God created woman, not
to be a distraction to the fellowship between man and
God, but rather to augment that relationship. Over time,
woman became the primary affection of a man, and
God's position of priority in the heart of a man was
diminished. It is a sad testament that today men are no
longer the priests of their households. That

responsibility has been relegated to the woman by default. This ought not to be so.

We are entering a time in history where the world desperately needs a correction to the misplaced biblical order of the family – a "righting" of the authority placed on men to truly be the head of their households and lead in a godly manner. This can only happen when intimate relationship is restored with God, the Father. This most effectively happens only *when a man worships.*

The writing of this book is inspired by the dreadful observation that when a man does not understand the purpose of worship or fails to actively engage in worship, that man, his family and his community suffer. This publication follows and accompanies a music CD I recorded, also entitled *When A Man Worships.* Each song title on the CD is represented by a same-titled chapter in the book. Chapters are introduced by thematically relevant lyrics from the corresponding song. A Bible verse, relevant to the topic to be discussed, is also presented to orient the reader. The experience of reading the book is optimally supplemented by simultaneous enjoyment of the songs that guided its writing. It is my prayer that both products compel men toward genuine and uninhibited worship that excites the heart of God and restores the communion that God and men seek.

Worship Defined

Worship is often one of the most misunderstood principles or acts of religious (or even spiritual) practice. The world broadly defines worship as the singing of songs or attendance at a religious gathering we call "church." While worship inspires these acts, the acts themselves do not define worship. Worship is not the sweet lyrics of a beautiful song about God, but worship can and does inspire the hand of the composer who pens the song. Worship is not the melodious noise that emanates from the voice of a gifted singer, but it inspires the heart-felt rendering of the song. The song itself is not worship. The act of singing the song is not worship. In fact, the assembling together in a facility to talk or sing about God is not worship. Worship is that which inspires these activities whether they be assembling, writing, singing, testifying or simply living according to God's statutes. Unfortunately, the true meaning of worship has been so badly misconstrued that in some churches worship is used to reference the slow songs we sing when we're exhausted from shouting and dancing in praise. It has become simply a moment to catch our breath and recuperate in preparation for the next "praise session." Such misperceptions and misunderstandings of worship render our experiences with God unmemorable and impotent.

In the Old Testament, an encounter with God always produced visible results. It engaged the attention and awe of all those who witnessed it. When Moses would enter the tent to worship, it would garner the attention and engagement of all the people who were around.

> *"... And it came about, whenever Moses went out to the tent, that all the people would arise and stand, each at the entrance of his tent, and gaze after Moses until he entered the tent. Whenever Moses entered the tent, the pillar of cloud would descend and stand at the entrance of the tent; and the LORD would speak with Moses. When all the people saw the pillar of cloud standing at the entrance of the tent, all the people would arise and worship, each at the entrance of his tent..." (Exod. 39:8-10).*

Worship that moves God, moves people. If our worship fails to inspire people to worship God themselves, then our worship is deficient. Some might propose that because Moses was the leader of his people, they were compelled to follow suit and worship whenever they saw him worship. Others might surmise that Moses was an exception and that because of the favor he had with God, he was endowed with a special anointing that allowed his worship to compel others to worship. While these arguments might have some truth, the reality is that the sacrifice of Christ has enabled each of us to have the same relationship with God that Moses had. While this was not possible in the Old Testament, we now have the privilege to establish such relationship directly with God, without needing a priest to be the intermediary. But still, we rely on others to cajole us to worship.

What is it then that made Moses' worship unique and special? The distinguishing feature of Moses' worship was relationship. A former pastor of mine, John W. Stevenson, defined a worshiper as "one who is intimately acquainted with and has a daily relationship with God." While I believe this is partially defines a worshiper, further study of the Bible allows us to expand this definition to incorporate the key prerequisite of obedience. Better defined, a worshiper would be "one who regularly communes with God through the daily practice of obedience and submission." In fact, obedience can be used synonymously with worship. Moses could not commune with God without obedience. He could not obey God without relationship – knowing who God is and surrendering to his sovereignty. While there have been hundreds, maybe thousands of books written on this subject – including this one – people still find it difficult to define and understand worship. Some of the other publications provide valuable details on the rituals of worship (both modern and historic). Others might outline the mechanisms and various expressions of worship. In all the discourse, we have complicated worship and made it difficult to understand. People are left now to wonder, what am I supposed to do to worship in a way that pleases God? Do I have to sacrifice bulls and goats as they did in the Old Testament? Do I need to raise my hands or sing a song? Should I close my eyes, speak in tongues, cry or remain silent? Worship is quite simple, which I hope to reveal in this publication. Worship is simply the mechanism by which we commune with God. Defined, worship is obedience and submission to the sovereignty of God which permits communion with God.

Worship that moves God, moves people.

Communion itself is not worship, rather, it is the product or outcome of worship. God desires communion with man, and worship allows communion to occur. God

6

doesn't desire worship because he is arrogant and narcissistic, needing man to inflate and nurture his ego. Rather, he seeks true worshipers because he desires to have communion with us (Exod. 24:1-22). One translation of the word communion, is "to speak." God desires to speak to man, much like he spoke with Adam, Moses and Abraham.

When God created man, he gave him dominion and freedom to access anything in the Garden of Eden. Adam and Eve were only forbidden to eat from the tree of knowledge of good and evil (Gen. 2:17). In Genesis 3, we see that as long as Adam remained obedient, God manifested himself to Adam in a way which He had never manifested himself to man before or since. The scripture suggests that God literally walked with Adam. When God spoke, Adam immediately heard. There were no obstacles standing between their relationship until Adam and Eve ate of the tree of the knowledge of good and evil. It was at that point that the relationship between God and man would forever be changed. Rather than commune with God uninhibited as he normally had, Adam now recognized his humanity and became ashamed. Prior to then, *"...the man and his wife were both naked and were not ashamed"* (Gen. 2:25). After eating the fruit, Adam didn't miraculously become more human than he previously was. However, his disobedience produced a knowledge of his humanness that was not previously present. This in turn produced

7

shame that separated him from continuous communion with God. In essence, disobedience produces separation between God and man.

Disobedience caused man to lose fellowship with God, but obedience (e.g., worship) allows the fellowship and communion with God to be restored. It was the disobedience of Adam and Eve that caused the separation. Because of that sin, God determined that in their human state, man should not live forever. He put man out of the Garden of Eden *"lest he reach out his hand and take also of the tree of life and eat, and live forever"* (Gen. 2:22). He went further to state that His *"Spirit shall not abide in man forever, for he is flesh..."* (Gen. 6:3). Man was made of flesh before he sinned. Because he became obedient to flesh after the sin, he could no longer have communion with God. Nonetheless, God still desired a mechanism whereby he could commune with man. He created worship to be that vehicle (Exod. 24:1-22).

Six hundred years after the fall of Adam, relationship with God was temporarily restored through the act of a single man, Noah. When the Earth dried after the flood, Noah's first action was to build an altar of burnt sacrifice. An offering of burnt sacrifice was presented as payment for sin. The aroma of this sacrifice rose unto the nostrils of God, who found it pleasing. This sacrifice compelled God to initiate a covenant again with man, specifically with Noah. The offering of sacrifice then became the mechanism by which man was restored to relationship with God. The sacrifice was a form of Old Testament worship that allowed God to again COMMUNE with man (Exod. 24:122). The process of sacrifice as a mechanism of worship was quite complicated. The practice was generally carried out by priests on behalf of people who, because of sin (or disobedience), had been separated from God. Because the ritual was so elaborate, it only occurred at certain times of the year. Though it was effective for the moment, communion with God was discontinuous. Between offerings, separation would occur again. Moreover, despite the sacrifice offered, God did not have communion with all men, only those chosen priests who would communicate what God would speak during times of communion. It was for this reason that God sent Jesus Christ, his only begotten Son, to be the ultimate sacrifice for sins. Through Jesus' sacrifice, the relationship with God could be restored on a continual basis and with any man who received Jesus' sacrifice as penance for his sin. *"For as by the one man's [Adam's] disobedience the many were made sinners, so by the one man's obedience [Jesus'] the many will be made righteous"* (Rom. 5:19).

Until Jesus, people had to rely on an intermediary, a priest, to speak to or hear from God (e.g., communion). It still required that the priest be made holy and that the people obeyed. For example, God would give instructions to Moses who would in turn convey them to the people. The response of the people was *"All the words that the Lord has spoken we will do"* (Exod. 19:3, 8). The prerequisite was obedience. Without obedience, there would be no worship and consequently no communion with God. There were only a few people in the Bible with whom God would have such intimate communion. Moses was clearly one, but another was Abraham.

Abraham had such special relationship with God, that God spoke with him as a man would speak with another man. This occurred because he embodied the essence of worship – obedience. When Abraham was instructed by God to sacrifice the thing that Abraham desired most, his son Isaac, he immediately obeyed without reservation or question. I consider this the ultimate act of obedience for several reasons. First, among his people, it was unheard of to offer your own child as a sacrifice. Further, this was the son of promise. God promised Abraham that he'd be the father of many nations. Isaac was the unexpected and miraculous conception of Abraham and his wife, Sarah, in their old age. Yet, when he received the command to make this great sacrifice, *"Abraham said to his young servants, 'Stay here with the donkey; I and the boy will go over there and worship and come again to you"* (Gen. 22:5). Abraham had confidence in knowing that both he and Isaac would "come again to" his servants. Although he

10

had no idea of how God would accomplish it, he had full assurance that God would still fulfill the promise of his legacy. Because his relationship with and trust in God was so strong, he was able to obey with the assurance that his obedience would produce a response from God – a response that would have the byproduct of blessing to Abraham. Certainly, God provided a ram for sacrifice as soon as Abraham raised the dagger to slay his own son in effort to worship (obey) God.

Worship is obedience and submission to the sovereignty of God which permits communion with God.

Based on the biblical references of worship described previously, it can be concluded that worship and obedience are synonymous. God desires more than any accoutrements of worship (e.g., songs, hand claps, adulation or bowed heads). He seeks obedience. Obedience is only accomplished when there is a healthy reverence for and submission to the sovereignty of God. When we recognize God as potentate, we willingly submit to his commands. The accoutrements of worship are important but should not be confused with worship itself. The reality is that God is already omnipotent. No song that we sing or action that we perform can ever make Him even the slightest bit bigger or more powerful

11

than He already is. Thus, the act of magnifying God is really the practice of making ourselves smaller in His presence. We bow in worship as a demonstration that we decrease, that He might be relatively increased in significance in our lives. John the Baptist demonstrated this well. As he was gaining in popularity, he was careful to remind the people that he was not the Christ and that *"He [Christ] must increase, but I must decrease"* (John 3:30). The singing of songs about the sovereignty of God only are worship when we are compelled by our embrace of the lyrics to humble ourselves before the King of Kings. The lifting of our hands become worship when, in our hearts, we offer the act as a demonstration of our surrender to the authority of an Almighty God. These expressions of worship are our modern-day fatlings. Just as God said that He preferred obedience over the sacrifice of fatlings, He prefers obedience over the mere act of raising our hands or bowing at our knees. While these postures may be demonstrations of gratitude or surrender, the key motive behind the demonstration is obedience and submission. True worship is a matter of the posture of a man's heart, not his body. The expressions of worship such as bowing or singing songs of reverence to a holy God are inspired by an internal acknowledgement of and surrender to the unquestioned and immutable sovereignty of God. When God is acknowledged as a sovereign king, obedience is inevitable. Disobedience, on the other hand, occurs in the presence of, and as evidence of, a personal challenge to God's sovereignty.

Disobedience produces separation between God and man.

When a man worships (obeys and submits to) God, God responds. If communion is the eventual goal of worship, it becomes immediately obvious when a man has ongoing communion with God. It manifests in the content of his speech and actions. Jesus said, *"...I say as the Father has told me"* (John 12:50) – so does the man who worships. When a man worships, he loves his wife as the Bible commands – *"as Christ loved the church and gave himself up for her, that he might sanctify her..."* (Eph. 5:25-26). When a man worships, he becomes the spiritual leader of his household, bringing his children *"up in the discipline and instruction of the Lord"* (Eph. 6:4). When a man worships, his steps are ordered by God, and his life is devoted to the fulfilling of his purpose in God.

YOU

"I will lift my hand. I'm totally surrendered to you – I'll just let it go. I don't care who's watching; you're the only one my heart beats for – You, I'll just let it show."

"... whoever would draw near to God must believe that he exists and that he rewards those who seek him" (Heb. 11:6).

The focus of worship must be God and an unadulterated desire for communion with Him. Unless you know who God is, you cannot effectively worship him. Jesus made this clear when He encountered the Samaritan woman at the well. On his arrival, Jesus asked this woman to give Him some water to drink (John 4:5-42). This was an opportunity for her to obey (e.g., worship) but she, not knowing who she was interacting with, responded contrary to that which was His desire. After some back and forth, she perceives that Jesus is a prophet. She then immediately wants to know if the worship she and her forefathers offered was effective (vs. 19). She asked Jesus if they are supposed to go to the mountains as her forefathers did or go to Jerusalem as the Jews say one should. Obviously, she had some confusion or misconception about what worship was supposed to look like. Her quest was to know whether her worship got to or was acceptable to God. In essence, she wondered whether her worship moved God. Jesus responded to her and said,

> *"You worship what you do not know; we worship what we know, for salvation is from the Jews. But the hour is coming and is now here, where the true worshipers will worship the Father in spirit and truth, for the Father is seeking such people to worship him. God is spirit, and those who worship him must worship in spirit and truth" (vs. 22-24).*

We worship what we know. In this statement, Jesus lays an important prerequisite for worship, and that is relationship. Worship that moves God is predicated on genuine relationship. This relationship was and is initiated by God. It started from the beginning when he created Adam but was perfected when he sent his son, Jesus. Though he was without sin, Jesus was sent to die on our behalf and for our sins so that relationship between man and God could be restored. Restoration of the relationship does not spontaneously happen. It starts with an invitation to relationship. Jesus said,

> *"Behold, I stand at the door and knock. If anyone hears my voice and opens the door, I will come in to him and eat with him, and he with me" (Rev. 3:20).*

The Lord is constantly knocking at the door of our hearts. However, before he can come in and allow me to get to know him, I must first hear the knocking and then respond by opening the door. This is obviously a figurative representation of our willingness to accept God into our hearts by accepting the sacrifice of Jesus Christ as remediation for our sin. We can't accept the sacrifice of Christ unless we first hear the invitation that offers.

For some reason, it seems difficult for men to hear the voice of God calling. I suspect it is in part because of our pride that forbids us from letting the world, or even people who are close to us, know that we do not have it all together. Perhaps it's a societal presumption that a man who shows weakness is undeserving of respect. In the animal kingdom, there is always a vying of males to achieve the position of dominance. Whether it's a pack of male lions trying to demark territorial boundaries or a male hippopotamus fighting for rights to mate with the herd of females, males seem to always seek unopposed dominion. A demonstration of dependence on someone, or some being, beyond ourselves can seemingly be a fatal weakness. We don't want or need help. We can fix it! All we need to do is give it a little more thought and a couple other tries and voila! Gentleman, no machination of man is able to fix a heart that is separated from God. The breech of relationship is mended only by relenting to the voice that calls to us in the quiet of the day or night – the voice that urges us to receive the redeeming love of Jesus Christ.

I assure you that it is acceptable to allow our humanity the freedom of being weak. There is a burden placed on men by society that we are incapable of managing one hundred percent of the time without some assistance, whether it comes from a human or spiritual source. Apostle Paul was a learned man who had some experiences about which he could easily boast and rightly be credited with some homage. He chose rather to not boast because he knew there were some things that were beyond his control. In 2 Corinthians 12, he rationalizes that the "thorn in his flesh" was placed there to keep him from gaining an over-inflated self-image. More importantly, it persisted so that he could hear the voice of God assuring him, *"My grace is sufficient for you, for my power is made perfect in weakness"* (vs. 9). As long as we fail to acknowledge our weakness, God's power in our lives remains imperfect. God desires to perfect His power in every aspect of our lives, but it requires that we willingly relent. Surrender is contrary to the nature that is within us because we always desire to dominate. Paul, being full of wisdom, determined *"Therefore I will boast all the more gladly of my weaknesses, so that the power of Christ may rest upon me. For the sake of Christ, then, I am content with weaknesses, insults, hardships, persecutions, and calamities. For when I am weak, then I am strong" (vs. 9-10).* The first step in knowing who God is, is an acknowledgement that He is the omnipotent God and that, in comparison to Him, we are weak. When we lift our hands and totally surrender to Him, his strength is then perfected in us.

When we acknowledge that He is God, and we are weak in our own might, we begin our quest for relationship with God. This journey quickly leads us to acceptance of the salvation He offers through Jesus Christ. Salvation is easily attained, not by good works, but by confessing that Jesus is Lord and believing in your heart that God raised Him from the dead (Rom. 10:9-10). Just as with any relationship, knowing a person doesn't occur immediately upon introduction. To genuinely know people, you must spend time with them and time listening to them. Listen to know the things they believe are important; what motivates them; what displeases them. What are their desires? Conveniently, all of this information about God is in writing. To know

God requires a continual and intentional study of his written word, the Bible. In so doing, we learn what drives or motivates God. We learn what disappoints Him. We learn about His behavior and how He responds when He is pleased or when He is disappointed. Often, we read the Bible and memorize verses out of religious routine. Sometimes, we do it for our own vain glory to demonstrate that we are "scholars of the word." When we instead study the Bible with the intent to better understand what moves God, we start to learn who He is and what His character is.

We also get to know God by spending time in prayer. Prayer is the way we make our requests known to God. I might have some biblical scholars disagree with me, but the primary purpose of prayer is not to commune with God. In believing they are the same, some confuse prayer with worship (e.g. communion), but prayer is clearly intended to petition God concerning a matter. This definition is supported by Philippians 4:6, *"do not be anxious about anything, but in everything by prayer and supplication with thanksgiving, let your requests be made known to God."* Further, Jesus gave us the best instruction for prayer in Matthew 6. His exemplary prayer started with an acknowledgement of who God is and of his greatness - "Our Father in heaven, hallowed be your name" (vs. 9). The remainder of the prayer consisted of petitions until he concluded with an acknowledgement that the kingdom, power and glory all belonged to God. Although, prayer is intended to be a supplication, we can still learn a lot about God through prayer. Sometimes we hit the mark with our petitions. Other times, we miss it widely. In so doing, we learn about the desires of God when those prayers are answered, or not. When they are not answered, we can discern that we have asked with the wrong motives - motives to fulfill our own pleasures as suggested in James 4:2 3. When they are answered, we learn that we are asking things that are within His will and timing. Through answered prayers, we come to know the compassion of God and how He loves to give good gifts to His children, when we ask with godly motives (Matt. 7:11). While prayer does provide some insight into who God is, it is not the key mechanism whereby get to know God. Spending time with Him and listening to Him, through communion and the study of His word, are much more instructive of who God is.

When we read God's word, we should study with the intent to know Him and to learn His voice. It takes a finely tuned ear to hear the voice of God. *"My sheep hear my voice, and I know them, and they follow me"* (John 10:27). When our relationship with God is tenuous, we are not confident whether the voice we hear is actually God. As our relationship grows, His voice becomes unmistakable. Importantly, in this passage of scripture, God affirms that He knows His sheep. While knowing God is important, it does not mean that we have a relationship with Him. I might know President Obama's voice, but it doesn't mean I have a relationship with him. However, when I know him, and he knows me, we have a relationship. In Genesis 33, God affirms that type of relationship with Moses. He speaks with Moses "face to face, as one speaks to a friend" (vs. 11) and commits to do the very thing that Moses asked because he found favor in God's sight and because God knew him "by name." That endorsement by God did not come because Moses did a lot of "good works" but rather because Moses was attentive to obey the voice of God and Moses reverenced the sovereignty of God.

A simple commitment to do good or even godly things is insufficient to build a relationship with God. A genuine "friendly" relationship with God is based on our commitment to obey the things God instructs. Jesus affirmed this when He advised his disciples that they would no longer be considered servants, but "friends" if they kept His commandments (John 15:14-15). Moses and Abraham were considered "friends" of God because they kept His commandments. Along this rationalization, one would presume that a failure to follow His instructions, or a decision to do good things of our own volition and later ascribe credit (or blame) to God for it, would disqualify us from relationship. This is suggested in Jesus' admonishment that

"Many will say to me in that day, Lord, Lord, have we not prophesied in thy name? And in thy name have cast out devils? And in thy name done many wonderful works? And then will I profess unto them, I never knew you: depart from me, ye that work iniquity" (Matt. 7:22-23, KJV).

As is made plain in this scripture, good or even honorable works do not constitute obedience. Consequently, they do not grant relationship or communion with God. Relationship or communion with God is permitted only through obedience and not necessarily sacrifice (I Samuel 15:22).

The fact of the matter is that Jesus declared that He would build His church on genuine relationship. In the sixteenth chapter of Matthew, Jesus has an interesting encounter with His disciples. He asked, "Who do people say that I am?" He first asked what his reputation among people who had no relationship with Him was. Their response was that some said that He was John the Baptist. Others said that He was Elijah, Jeremiah or one of the prophets. The response of the "people" made evident that they didn't know who Jesus was. Jesus then asked the disciples, "But who you say that I am?" It is unclear if the other disciples had a revelation of who Jesus was, but Simon Peter replied, "You are the Christ, the Son of the living God." Because Peter was the only one who answered in this manner might suggest that even the other disciples who had been with Jesus had not been close enough to Him to have a full revelation of who He was. Jesus responded to Peter and called him blessed because flesh and blood did not reveal it to him, but God who is in heaven did. The reality is that we can't get a revelation of who Jesus is unless it is released by God. Just as God granted Peter eyes to see who Jesus was, He also grants us the clarity to see Him. However, this comes only through constant observation of who Jesus is and listening to the words He speaks. Because Jesus is not walking on the earth today, we rely on the written word of God.

While it was good that Peter had a revelation from God about Jesus' identity, the revelation was not the thing upon which Jesus said He would build his church After Peter demonstrated that he knew who Jesus was, Jesus replied, *"And I tell you, you are Peter and on this rock, I will build my church, and the gates of hell shall not prevail against it"* (Matt. 16:18). Jesus was saying because you know who I am and more importantly, I can say that I know you, we are in covenant relationship. It is upon the covenantal relationship between man and God that Jesus will build His church. When Jesus can say, "I know Mark" just as he said, "I know Peter" or as God said, "I know Abraham and Moses", He can build a strong church that cannot be destroyed. When Jesus knows who I am – we have genuine relationship – I

24

don't have to worry about the works that I do in His name being called works of iniquity. Instead, He will respond the same way he responded to Peter when he said, *"I will give you the keys of the kingdom of heaven, and whatever you bind on earth shall be bound in heaven, and whatever you loose on earth shall be loosed in heaven"* (vs. 19). You don't let someone with whom you don't have intimate relationship have keys to your home or to your kingdom. You don't delegate authority to someone who you don't know and who doesn't know you. But when we have covenantal relationship with God through Jesus, we can be endued with power to bind or loose on earth, the things that are bound or loosed in heaven.

Communion with God cannot happen unless we first know who God is and as importantly have God know us by name. When we establish intimate relationship with Him through the study of His word and spending time in His presence through prayer, we learn to trust Him. We learn to submit to his sovereignty and grow more confident in the safety of obedience and surrender to Him. *When a man worships,* his focus is on God, and the passion of his heart becomes, "How can I please YOU, God?" He will lift his hands unashamed, not intimidated by those who might be spectators or critics. He will totally surrender his desires to be influenced only by the God who is the object of his passion and affection. When a man is attentive to observe the statutes of God and is not distracted by the promise of an inferior love offered by the world, the benefits of that submission manifests in very clear and measurable ways. Most notably, it solicits the "God endorsement" that not only does the man know God, but God also knows the man – the hallmark of true relationship. He will recognize that the love of his woman and the allure of riches or fame pale in comparison to the love of God which is indeed deeper than the sea. The love of God makes his heart beat and his soul sing. To God, he'll exclaim, "the preeminent consumer of my attention is YOU!"

DON'T LET ME STRAY

"All I want to do is spend more time with you. Whatever's on your heart, let it be on mine."

"Cast me not away from your presence, and take not your Holy Spirit from me. Restore to me the joy of your salvation and uphold me with a willing spirit"
(Ps. 51:11-12).

Worship is the vehicle through which we commune with God. As mentioned in previous chapters, it requires relationship and obedience. However, it also requires repentance and commitment to uphold the statutes and principles of God. Repentance is simply a sorrowful acknowledgement of wrongdoing and a turning away from sin. Both components are necessary.

Without turning away from the sin, the acknowledgement is simply a confession. Worship helps us not only turn away from the sin, but it also helps us stay away from the sin. Paul encouraged believers to "Stand fast therefore in the liberty wherewith Christ hath made us free, and be not entangled again with the yoke of bondage" (Gal. 5:1). When we are set free, we must remain free and not be tempted to go back to or be drawn back into the life from which we were delivered. To do this, we must guard our hearts and minds against temptations and distractions that easily ensnare us.

David was considered a man after God's own heart. It didn't mean that he was without sin. Rather, it meant that David knew how to acknowledge his sin and quickly find his way back to right standing with God. David actually committed sins that would likely make most of us cringe. He slept with another man's wife and got her pregnant. To cover up his sin, he sent the husband out to battle on the front line to be killed so that his sin wouldn't be discovered. What makes David different is not that he sinned, but that he never became comfortable with or in his sin. Rather, in great sorrow and with sincere regret, he petitioned the Lord for forgiveness and committed to turn away from that sin. He understood that the *"sacrifices of God are a broken spirit: a broken and a contrite heart"* (Ps. 51:17, KJV). He pleaded with God,

"Wash me thoroughly from mine iniquity, and cleanse me from my sin. For I acknowledge my transgressions: and my sin is ever before me. Against thee, thee only, have I sinned, and done this evil in thy sight..." (vs. 2-4).

David knew that his sin would bring an end to his communion with God, so he begged, "Create in me a clean heart, O God; and renew a right spirit within me. Cast me not away from thy presence; and take not thy Holy Spirit from me" (vs. 10-11). His ultimate desire was to remain in close relationship with God. David knew that his only hope for success and contentment was through unencumbered communion with God.

Because David recognized the necessity and the benefit of close communion with God, he approached God with sincere contrition. From his youth, David knew that as long as he was in right standing with God, he would never be forsaken (Ps. 37:25). He believed that if he delighted himself in the Lord that he would be granted the desires of his heart. If he committed his ways unto the Lord and trusted Him then anything he needed, God would provide (vs. 4-5). Whether it was protection from evildoers or provision of food, peace or shelter, God would provide it if David remained faithful. Some might read this and surmise that David was being manipulative and that he remained faithful to God only for the benefits. It is evident that this was not his motive.

David understood that the benefits of a relationship with God were the byproduct of his worship and not the impetus for it. God, who searches the hearts of man, also knows the motive for our worship. He consequently knew David's heart and found it to be genuinely repentant. For that reason, God withheld no good thing from David in spite of his failures (Ps. 84:11).

Blessings are the byproduct of unadulterated worship, not the impetus.

As a side note, we cannot con God into blessing us. When our worship is pure and acceptable to him, God's natural inclination is to bless us. Because we are made in His image, we do the same thing. When a person's behaviors toward us are pleasing, we are more inclined to bless him or her. However, God is much better at discerning the con than we are. Imagine if your child cozied up next to you and proceeded to tell you how great you are and how much he loves you. He recounts how grateful he is for all that you've done for him and asserts that there is no one he would rather spend time with or be like more than you. You've gotten so softened by the many kind words he spoke that you are ready and willing to give him almost anything he wants. And then he asks you for $150 to go to the mall. In that moment, you have to question whether all of the words he previously spoke were genuine, or if they were intended to con you out of your money. Perhaps both of the motives inspired the encounter. But you're left wondering because you don't truly know what was in his heart. God does know, and he still called David a man after his own heart. Even though David understood the benefits of worship, his communion with God was never motivated by a desire to get a blessing from God. He recognized that blessings are the byproduct of unadulterated worship, not the impetus. Apparently, he was so enamored with the character of God, that he could easily forget that a relationship has its privileges. In fact, at one point he had to encourage himself to not forget the many benefits of a right relationship with God (Ps. 103), which suggests that the benefits were not at the forefront of his mind. Because the benefits of relationship with God are plentiful, we must intentionally guard against the blessing becoming a distraction from the relationship.

Distractions occur during both hardship or prosperity. They can present themselves as blessings or temptations. It is imperative that we have the ability to quickly identify them and definitively squash them. Otherwise, it is easy for us to wander from the path of righteousness. A common distraction for men is the workplace. As men, we rightly feel an obligation to provide for our households. The Bible tells us that the man who fails to provide for his family is actually worse than an unbeliever (I Tim. 5:8). In our pursuit of provision and worldly possessions, we sometimes deprioritize our relationship with family and even God. We begin making the sacrifices that were never requested by God or our spouses to achieve the carnally laudable goal of financial independence. I've seen too many marriages destroyed due to the misconception that the man who is consumed with working and earning money does it as a sacrifice for his spouse and children. This is usually the man's fallacy. His wife has a different testimony. Undoubtedly, the commitment of hours at work is a sacrifice. However, the sacrifices are futile because they may not be what was requested and consequently serve no real purpose other than to distract our attention from the sacrifice that is required. It doesn't matter how honorable the sacrifice might be, if it is not the one that is requested, it is simply a distraction.

The concept of futile sacrifices became evident to me during medical school. With the pressures of school and trying to be an outstanding husband and father (of two children), I would often find myself needing to go fishing to be rejuvenated. One Saturday morning, I desperately needed one of these retreats but determined that since I had been absent for most of the week, I needed to stay at home. Now, keep in mind that neither my wife nor children requested that I not go fishing; it was my own "discernment." After a full day of doing absolutely nothing of much meaning around the house, I later in frustration mentioned the sacrifice I made and how I really wanted (or needed) to go fishing that day. My wife's response was, "I didn't ask you to not go." And, indeed, she hadn't. She would have been just as content if I had gone fishing that day as she was when I stayed home. It was a sacrifice because it cost me something to offer. At the same time, it was futile because it wasn't her request and consequently was of little value to her. What has always mattered more is my willingness to provide the things that she actually asks for – the things that are most meaningful to her. We can so exhaust ourselves offering futile sacrifices that when it is time to make the sacrifice that is requested, we have little or no enthusiasm for offering it.

Saul attempted to make a futile sacrifice unto God. God told Saul to *"...smite Amalek, and utterly destroy all that they have, and spare them not; but slay both man and woman, infant and suckling, ox and sheep, camel and ass"* (I Sam. 15:3). Saul was disobedient to what God commanded. He smote the Amalekites, but spared King Agag, and the best of the sheep, oxen, fatlings, lambs and all that was good (vs. 9). When confronted by the prophet Samuel about his disobedience, he offered the weak excuse that the "people" spared all that was good to sacrifice unto God. Samuel's response was *"...hath the Lord as great delight in burnt offerings and sacrifices, as in obeying the voice of the Lord? Behold, to obey is better than sacrifice, and to hearken than the fat of rams"* (vs. 22).

There is a sacrifice that God desires. It is a sacrifice of obedience, and obedience has a cost. It costs the relinquishment of your own desires, ideas and aspirations. Saul anticipated that it would be wasteful to sacrifice all of the goods of the Amalekites. Besides, it was custom that the winner of a battle kept the spoils. Surely, it would seem better to offer the highest quality portion of these spoils as a sacrifice to God than to needlessly waste them. I can imagine these must have been some of the things running through Saul's mind. If he had offered them to God, they would have been futile sacrifices because they weren't what He requested. While there was a time and place for burnt offerings, it was not the offerings themselves that were the atonement. It was the obedience to the process that was important to God. As men, we ought not present God or our spouses with the sacrifices we determine are most appropriate. Rather, we should offer the sacrifice that is requested. Anything other than that is a distraction. These distractions are the things that redirect our attention from following through with the assigned task. Distractions are the predecessors of disobedience and futility. When indulged, they pull us away from our pursuit of relationship with God and may be harmful for our families.

While the pursuit of riches is a common distraction, we must also beware of the distraction of women. Solomon, the wisest man to ever live, warned his son to remember the wife of his youth and to always be satisfied with only her breasts (Prov. 5:18-19). Solomon likely used the breasts as an object of instruction for his son for multiple reasons. The most obvious is that breasts of a woman are one of the more alluring physical traits of a woman. According to the American Society of Plastic Surgeons, Americans spend $16.5 billion dollars each year on cosmetic surgery, and the vast majority of this is spent on breast augmentation. Men know it, and women know! That's why they spend so much money on augmentation. Attractive breasts easily garner the attention of even the most well-intentioned and disciplined man – at least for a moment. Solomon admonished his son to not be easily drawn to the physical attributes of a woman, except it be his own wife's. He should be intentional to admire and be satisfied with only his wife's inward and outward beauty. More than an ornament of sexual attraction, the breasts are instrumental in a woman's ability to nurture. When she has given birth, the breasts are a source of nutrition for an infant. More importantly, the skin to skin contact of a nursing child helps an infant and parent bond more readily than bottle feeding. Obviously, a man doesn't need bottle feeding. However, the breasts still symbolically represent the ability of a woman to nurture.

A man who might not so easily be influenced by a woman's outward beauty, might easily be drawn in by her ability to nurture the emotional or psychological void that a man might have. Solomon was wise to advise his son to stand guard against allowing himself to be emotionally or physically drawn to a woman other than his wife.

Distractions are the predecessors of disobedience and futility.

It is tempting to look into your neighbor's yard to determine the greenness of their grass rather than tending to the lawn of your own home. I recall a dream I had when I was about 20 years old. In the dream, there was a power or force that would "pull great men down" into the ground. If the force were obvious at the outset men, would easily have resisted it. However, the touch of the force was gentle and soft – one that was pleasing to the senses. Once a man succumbed to the tender touch, it immediately transformed into a rough and powerful twig-like structure that pulled him down into the ground, resulting in his destruction.

As I was studying the Bible a year later, I came across Proverbs 7. In this passage, the writer described a woman who is cunningly seductive. A man, with little understanding of the destruction that awaits him, would yield to her fair speech and flattery. Solomon admonished his son,

> *"Let not your heart turn aside to her ways; do not stray into her paths, for many a victim has she laid low and all her slain are a mighty throng. Her house is the way to Sheol, going down to the chambers of death" (Prov. 7:25-27).*

God has provided ample warning for men to avoid the trap of believing that you can dip your foot in the water and not get wet. Ravi Zacharias said, "sin will take you farther than you want to go, keep you longer than you want to stay, and cost you more than you want to pay." This seems particularly true with men and sexual sin.

Throughout the Bible, there are many examples to illustrate the notion that a man's greatest susceptibility is a woman. Adam ate of forbidden fruit because he was tempted to by the woman, not the serpent. Even though David was a consummate worshiper and had a harem of wives and concubines, he still was drawn to Bathsheba. With her, he committed his great sin against God. Samson lost his strength and favor with God because of his susceptibility to a woman. Even today, there are many great men and presidents who have fallen victim to the temptation of a woman. We must remain vigilant to protect our hearts and our bodies against situations wherein we are easily tempted by women. Joseph provides an excellent example of how to guard against this type of distraction.

Joseph was greatly envied by his brothers. As a result, they sold him into slavery and told his parents that he was killed by a wild animal. While Joseph was enslaved to Potiphar, he excelled in everything he did. Potiphar could tell that God favored Joseph and eventually made him the administrator over all of his affairs. The Bible says that *"Joseph was a very handsome and well-built young man, and Potiphar's wife soon began to look at him lustfully. 'Come and sleep with me,' she demanded. But Joseph refused:*

"'Look,' he told her, 'my master trusts me with everything in his entire household. No one here has more authority than I do. He has held back nothing from me except you, because you are his wife. How could I do such a wicked thing? It would be a great sin against God'" (Gen. 39:6-9).

Potiphar's wife continued day after day to entice Joseph, and he continued to refuse. To avoid the temptation, he stayed as far away from her as he could. One day, however, as he was working, Potiphar's wife came close to Joseph when no one was around. She grabbed his clothes and demanded that he sleeps with her. Joseph quickly ran from her, but in doing so, his clothes tore. The wife then screamed to gain attention and accused Joseph of raping her.

I did say that Joseph was a good example of how to avoid the temptation, and he is – even though he was wrongfully accused of rape. Here's why. In this passage of scripture, we discover key strategies to avoid the pit of sexual immorality. First, Joseph knew his worth. One of the reasons he was so despised by his siblings was because he shared a dream with them wherein God showed him that he would one day rule over all of them. He was also favored by his father because he was the long-awaited first child born to Rachel, Jacob's favorite wife. He did not allow his misfortune of being betrayed by his brothers, thrown into a pit and sold into slavery change his perspective of what God called him to be. He saw the brightness his future offered and refused to let any circumstance or distraction keep it from being manifested. Second, Joseph knew and respected his boundaries. He was given charge over all that Potiphar had, except his wife. Joseph knew that the penalty for adultery could be death. More importantly, he knew that the benefits he obtained from honoring and being in communion with God were much greater than any benefit obtained from his moment of pleasure with Potiphar's wife.

Gaining wealth and authority can be a blessing and a trap. There is an inherent trap in being able to obtain all that you want. When your resources are limited, you will likely refrain from certain indulgences because you have no other option. But when you have all that you *need*, the capacity to obtain all that you *want* can be a snare. It is wise to routinely practice denying yourself of desires and whims, even when it is not necessary. Not everything you desire is sinful. But when you have the financial capacity to obtain almost anything you want, it becomes increasingly important to practice self-denial. The unencumbered practice of obtaining all that you desire, strengthens the flesh. Practicing intentional self-denial, even for things that are not necessarily harmful, makes the flesh subject to boundaries. Apart from this practice, carnal desires will predominate. Although Joseph had power and authority – likely more than a slave would ordinarily have – he trained his flesh to respect the boundaries placed before him.

The third observation we should make is that Joseph acknowledged God in his situation. He recognized that if he had slept with his master's wife, not only would he have dishonored himself, his future and his master, but more importantly he would have dishonored God. Proverbs 3:6 admonishes us to acknowledge God in all our ways, and He will direct or straighten our paths. Most of the time we only want to acknowledge God in our "good" ways, not realizing that God is still aware of our misgivings. He desires to be acknowledged or consulted even in our "bad" ways so that he can make the crooked path we're taking straight again. The word acknowledge, in this context means to perceive or to respect God in all of our ways. Rather than doing such a dishonorable thing, Joseph perceived that God was present and deserved greater respect for His sovereignty and His goodness toward Joseph. Fourthly, Joseph was clear and vocal about his denial. He did not hedge around the point or indulge her behavior by being flattered. He knew what he was not going to do, and he said it plainly. He also gave an honorable reason why he refused to engage. He didn't conditionalize the denial by saying, "if I weren't married" or something similar. He said plain and simply, "I can't, and I won't do this thing and dishonor God."

If we were to be honest, we sometimes like to indulge some of the flattery we receive from women – especially if we're older and/or have been married for long time. We like to believe that "we still got it!" We all like to feel that we are still attractive. The Bible says that Joseph was attractive and well-built. It was probably not difficult for Potiphar's wife to recognize that. Maybe Joseph already knew he had it going on. Even if he didn't, or if he questioned whether he still had it, he did not allow his insecurity to jeopardize his future. Don't let these young women fool you! If they think you got it going on, you'd better keep them moving on.

This brings me to the fifth tactic Joseph used to avoid the distraction of temptation. He avoided situations where he or she would be tempted. Joseph continued with the work that he was required to do, but he avoided her and any potential opportunity where they might have been alone. Brothers, don't fool yourself into thinking that you are strong enough to be in that situation and not fall. Remember, when Jesus was tempted by the devil to prove His power, He replied, *"Thou shalt not tempt the Lord thy God"* (Matt. 4:7, KJV). If Jesus passed up the opportunity to display His power, you and I certainly should not test our will-power by putting ourselves in that position. In fact, I encourage you to say exactly what Jesus said, in the King James Version – which makes it more holy. I'm just kidding. Nonetheless, the point remains that if Jesus wouldn't do it, we should not tempt fate because eventually we will fail.

When you have all that you need, the capacity to obtain all that you want can be a snare.

Finally, you might find yourself in a circumstance that could not be avoided, or that was avoidable but foolishly was indulged. In this predicament, Joseph demonstrated the final tactic to avoid the temptress. He ran! When you can't avoid the situation, run and run quickly. Remove yourself from the situation before it gets to the point where you may potentially be unable to resist the temptation. I'm not sure what Joseph thought at the moment he ran but surely at some point, he realized that he might have to see her again and deal with the embarrassment of his expedient departure. In that moment, that wasn't his concern, nor should it be yours. There is greater embarrassment in falling into the temptation than there is in running from it. In this case, even though Joseph ran, he was still accused and thrown into jail. While that was a less than ideal outcome, Joseph remained encouraged because he knew that he continued to obey and honor God. He continued to worship which kept his communion with God open. As long as you maintain satisfactory communion with God, the blessings will continue to flow, and they did for Joseph. *"The Lord was with Joseph and showed him steadfast love and gave him favor in the sight of the keeper of the prison"* (Gen. 39:21). Because of his steadfastness, Joseph was eventually released and became ruler over all of Egypt – second in power only to Pharaoh (Gen. 41:40-41). Joseph's destiny was fulfilled only because he intentionally avoided the distractions that sought to separate him from communion with God.

Like David and Joseph, a man who worships will constantly pray, "Lord, don't let me stray away." He remembers the necessity and the benefits of constant communion with God. He stays defensively alert to distractions that this world offers to pull him away from relationship with God. Before he consents to sin, he will hear a voice within him cry like Joseph did saying, *"How then can I do this great wickedness and sin against God?"* (Gen. 39:9).

Sins against God extend beyond those of a sexual or lustful nature. They also include any distraction from offering the sacrifice that God requests. Even the things that we would consider laudable sacrifices become abominable because they are exercises in futility and are birthed in disobedience. Moreover, futile sacrifices and disobedience separate us from communion with God. In contrast, worship (obedience), keep us closely connected to the Father, who keeps us from falling, and brings us to the expected end that God has predestined for us.

WANNA BE USED

"I just wanna be used by you, Oh God. I'm willing to do whatever you want me to."

"Then I heard the voice of the Lord saying, "Whom shall I send? And who will go for us?" And I said, "Here am I. Send me!" (Isa. 6:8).

The work of discipleship is not easy but will be the most meaningful and eternal thing you'll ever do. We spend much of our time doing things that will have only a temporal or short-lived benefit. However, when we avail ourselves to be used by God, the results are everlasting. Men are often absent from the battlefield of evangelism, and women seem to do the lion's share of work. Women are often more committed to winning souls for Christ and helping to shoulder the work of ministry in the church. The list of potential reasons is plentiful. However, none of them are sufficient to justify the curious absence of men in the church's effort to reap the harvest of souls.

Preparation to share the testimony is evidenced by the fact that the thing that once held you captive, no longer has influence over you.

One reason men might be absent in service to God is a feeling of being ill-prepared. While it is true that it is important for every believer to be well-prepared and learned in the scriptures, this benefit is mainly for the person who is sharing the message, not the one hearing it. By that, I mean the Gospel message that we share to proselytize is quite simple. We hear the scripture, *"Study to shew thyself approved unto God, a workman that needeth not be ashamed, rightly dividing the word of truth"* (2 Tim. 2:15, KJV) and are intimidated at times because of our lack of scriptural proficiency. The Gospel message simply is God loves you; Jesus died for you, and Jesus rose again so you could be free from sin. It does not require an exhaustive exegesis or a hermeneutical exposition of the scriptures – whatever that means. It involves the simple conveyance of how great God's love is for the lost and how simple it is to be made whole. Besides, there is no evangelistic message that is more compelling than the telling of your own story.

The Bible tells us that *"... they overcame him [the devil] by the blood of the Lamb, and by the word of their testimony; and they loved not their lives unto the death"* (Rev. 12:11). Each of us has a story about how we came to Jesus. The simple sharing of this story draws others to the love of Christ. However, it requires that we be unashamed of our testimony. This passage in Revelation qualifies the testimony by saying, "they loved not their lives unto the death." Simply put, to be effective, they had to abandon any concern they had about their reputations, societal status or even the safety of their very lives. Like them, any of these concerns could easily cause you or me to hold back our testimony – a testimony that might be the key to someone else's liberty.

The Gospel message simply is God loves you; Jesus died for you, and Jesus rose again so you could be free from sin.

When the children of Israel were preparing to move into the Promised Land, after wandering in the desert for 40 years, God instructed Joshua to prepare the people because the next day they would possess the land (Josh. 3). Joshua did exactly as the Lord instructed him to do. The priests led the way. As soon as their feet hit the brink of the flooded waters of the Jordan river, the waters parted and allowed the people to pass over on dry land (vs. 15-17). A key event happened after they crossed. The Lord told Joshua to take twelve "prepared" men – one from each tribe of Israel. He commanded them to go back into the water where the priests stood on dry ground. Each one would take a stone from that place, put it on his shoulder and carry it into Jericho where they lodged after crossing the river (Josh. 4:2-3). After they returned to dry land, they were instructed to erect the stones to form a memorial which would serve as a testimony to their children in generations to come. When the children of subsequent generations would ask what the memorial represented, the elders would share how the Lord faithfully brought them out of the bondage of Egypt and into their promised land.

I believe the stones from the Jordan river represented an individual testimony. The men who were instructed to go back to get the stones had to be "prepared" men. The Hebrew word for prepared is "kuwn." It means to be firm, stable or established (Strong's Exhaustive Concordance). These men needed to be able to withstand any current that could sweep them away as they went back into the water.

Importantly, these men needed to be established men – men who could be trusted and who were firm in their loyalty and foundation. If the stones are representative of a testimony, it is important for us to be stable and established before we go back to get our stones. What do I mean by that? Everyone is not prepared to share his or her testimony. Preparation to share the testimony is evidenced by the fact that the thing that once held you captive, no longer has influence over you. You can't testify of the goodness of God to bring you through or out of a situation, if He hasn't already done it or if you're still struggling in it. In this case, you are not "prepared" to testify. If you are still condemned by it or continue to carry shame for the mistakes of your past, you are not prepared to testify. It is noteworthy that God didn't tell the men to gather the stones as they crossed over the river the first time. He told them after they had already completely and safely crossed the river, to go back and get the testimony. See, a testimony is only a testimony when you have been completely delivered. The sharing of your story before you are completely freed is not a testimony; it is a confession. To render life-changing testimony, you must be fully delivered, firm, stable and established.

As previously mentioned, if you still love your life and/or your reputation too much, you will be ineffective in providing testimony that causes others to overcome. I believe the prepared men were instructed to carry the stones on their shoulders so they could be plainly visible. When someone saw the man's face, they saw the stone. The stone was not hidden but displayed in plain sight. The same occurs with effective testimony. Our testimonies should not be hidden or dissociated from who we are, our stature or our reputation. Often, we prefer to hide the testimony behind our backs or carry it in a wheelbarrow so that no one knows whose testimony it really is. However, a yoke-destroying testimony should not and cannot be hidden. It is presented unashamedly and directly relates to your personal story. If we truly believe that *"there is therefore now no condemnation for those who are in Christ Jesus"* (Rom. 8:1), we can readily tell the whole testimony of what God has brought us through. When we are able to do this, those who hear the testimony can overcome by hearing it and by the blood of the Lamb.

The sharing of your story before you are completely freed is not a testimony; it is a confession.

It is easy for some of us to feel as if we have failed so many times or that our failure was so great that God couldn't possibly use us. There is an old song by Ron Kenoly that says, "If you can use anything, Lord, you can use me. Take my hands, Lord, and my feet. Touch my heart, Lord, speak through me. If you can use anything, Lord, you can use me." More than lyrics of a popular song, these are proclamations of surrender. It is often said that God doesn't call the qualified; he qualifies the called.

Throughout the scriptures, God used the least likely of people to accomplish his will. For example, David was the least likely, among all his brothers, to have been chosen to succeed King Saul. He was a scrawny kid while his other brothers were much statelier and outwardly appeared much kinglier than David. But God reminded Samuel that *"... the Lord sees not as man sees: man looks on the outward appearance, but the Lord looks on the heart"* (I Sam. 16:7). As another example, Moses stuttered or had some other communication disorder that affected his articulation and the intelligibility of his speech. He almost let this handicap disqualify him from God's use (Exod. 4:10-17). In fact, his self-consciousness about his speech kindled the anger of the Lord. Although God had the power to miraculously cure his speech impediment and his apprehensions about it, God instead chose to use him despite his deficiency and insecurities. God sent Moses' brother, Aaron, along with him to be his mouthpiece. God's purpose is always greater than your inadequacy. If He doesn't remedy your inadequacy, He will use it to obtain glory in the most unlikely way.

51

I can relate to Moses' being self-conscious about his speech impediment. As a child and even throughout high school, I was terrified to speak in public or even in the classroom. I vividly remember, in the 11th grade, being too bashful to ask to be excused to the restroom. I was self-conscious about the tone of my voice, in part because I was taunted by my brothers about it. I would watch the second hand on the clock and encourage myself, "When the second hand gets on the 12, then raise your hand and ask." With nervous anticipation, I'd watch the second hand go from 7 to 8, 9, 10, 11 and 12. Then I'd watch it go from 1 to 2, then 3, 4 or 5 and have to start the ritual all over again, until it became an unavoidable necessity that I overcome my fear. When my bladder got full enough, I'd have no choice but to either embarrass myself from wetting my pants or by being heard. Now, I am a public speaker, worship leader and recording artist. As much as I talk, no one would ever believe that I was afraid to be heard asking something as simple as to be excused to the restroom, in front of a class full of 20 or so of my peers.

God's purpose is always greater than your inadequacy. If He doesn't remedy your inadequacy, He will use it to obtain glory in the most unlikely way.

Now, as a voice doctor, I understand the importance of a voice in everyday life. The voice is important for communication and identification. As a man of God and a man who worships, I recognize an even greater spiritual importance of the voice. Residing within our voices is the power to move mountains; to speak life or death; to establish foundations. The play of the devil, however, is to keep God's people silent – to keep men silent. His strategy is always first to say, "No one wants to hear what you have to say; what could you possibly say that would be of benefit; you are not qualified to speak on this" or something similar.

We don't have to be the most eloquent orator to impact the lives of people around us. We just need to have the courage to open our mouths and proclaim the testimony of God. Paul said it well:

> *"And I, when I came to you, brothers, did not come proclaiming to you the testimony of God with lofty speech or wisdom. For I decided to know nothing among you except Jesus Christ and him crucified. And I was with you in weakness and in fear and much trembling, and my speech and my message were not in plausible words of wisdom, but in demonstration of the Spirit and of power, so that your faith might not rest in the wisdom of men but in the power of God" (I Cor. 2:1-5).*

We err when we are more concerned about how we might look or sound, rather than how God might look. In essence, Paul was saying, "I might have been trembling in fear and stumbling over my words, but that doesn't matter. I don't want you to put your faith in my or any other man's wisdom but instead in the power of God." We should never desire to receive glory for the work we do for Christ. Glory is intended to be reflected – not absorbed. Glory absorbed by man is toxic. When we try to receive the glory for God's work, we predispose ourselves to toxicity and failure. On the contrary, when it is reflected toward God, those who are lost will see it and will follow the light to God.

Glory is intended to be reflected – not absorbed. Glory absorbed by man is toxic.

When a man worships, he avails his life – the good, the bad and the ugly; the future, present and past – to be used in any manner God sees fit. When he worships (obeys) God he transitions from a place of self-centeredness to surrender. When a life is surrendered, concern about reputation and personal advancement or status dissipates. When he is no longer condemned by his past or controlled by the threat of future reputational damage, he is prepared to share a life-changing testimony that causes others to overcome. His testimony is not squelched by the enemy's falsehoods and taunting, which only attempt to silence the freedom he holds in his tongue. He is free to speak of the goodness of God, and in so doing, he liberates those who would hear.

FREE AT LAST

*"It didn't matter where I'd be, trouble always
seemed to find me and succeed to bring me to my
knees. There I made this earnest plea, would
someone come rescue me? Find a way to finally set
me free."*

*"Blessed is the man who walks not in the counsel of
the wicked, nor stands in the way of sinners, nor sits
in the seat of scoffers; but his delight is in the law of
the Lord, and on his law he meditates day and
night. He is like a tree planted by streams of water
that yields its fruit in its season, and its leaf does not
wither. In all that he does, he prospers"* (Ps. 1:1-3).

What thoughts predominate in your mind
throughout the day? Are they selfish and self-
centered thoughts? Are the thoughts directed first at
what pleases you? While it is easy for any man to be
consumed by his own selfishness, it is especially true for
unmarried men or those who have no children. It is even

a sadder discourse when it can be said of the man who is married and who has children. I would not dare paint with such a broad stroke to state that most men are self-centered because there are so many men who spend a good percentage of their time thinking about their spouse and children and how they can provide for them. While this is laudable and necessary, later discussed, it still isn't the ultimate goal – though it is part of it.

When a man worships, his mind stays on God. The man with this mind derives blessings from God. As mentioned in an earlier chapter, blessings are the byproduct of, not the impetus for, worship. When a man delights in keeping the law of the Lord, he worships – he obeys. He obeys because the law of the Lord is constantly on his mind. Now, I don't mean to suggest that a very ritualistic or legalistic recitation of the Ten Commandments should predominate a man's thoughts. Rather, a man who worships focuses on how his actions and words will please (or displease) the Lord. In Genesis 39, Joseph had been given great power in Potiphar's house and was seduced by Potiphar's wife to engage sexually with her. Rather than indulge the thought of it, his response was *"How then can I do this great wickedness and sin against God?"* (vs. 9).

If we were honest about it, most of us in a similar situation, might have as our first thought, "What if I get caught?" – especially if the woman is attractive or powerful. Those of us that are more contemplative will carry the scenario out further and ask (at least in today's environment), "what if she gets pregnant? What if I catch a sexually transmitted disease? What if her husband finds out? What if she uses this to blackmail me?" A variety of scenarios might flood our minds, if we're lucky. And, if we have a modicum of integrity, these potential scenarios might stop us from committing the act of sin not just against ourselves, the woman and our own spouse (if we're married), but more importantly against God.

Joseph's preeminent concern was not about the practical consequences of getting caught. Certainly, he would've lost his job, reputation and likely his life if he had committed this act and gotten caught. Despite his exercise of restraint, he was accused by Potiphar's wife of committing the act even though he refused. He quickly found himself imprisoned for an act he never committed. Since, his mind was focused on God and how he might please the Lord, God caused him to gain favor even while in jail. *"Whatever he did, the Lord made it succeed"* (Gen. 39:23). It would be at least two years of being imprisoned before Joseph would have the opportunity to be vindicated. His reputation of being a virtuous man who communed with God presented him the opportunity to interpret Pharaoh's troubling dreams. It was after accurately interpreting the dreams that Pharaoh promoted Joseph to oversee all of Egypt, and asked,

"Can we find a man like this, in whom is the Spirit of God?" (Gen. 41:38). The Spirit of God's habitation within a man earmarks that man for greatness and for blessing. Joseph's obedience to God positioned him for a blessing. Though he was imprisoned, his worship of God caused him to nonetheless be free and prosperous.

Obedience to the will of God does not spontaneously occur. It happens only through the continual meditation on the word of God. This doesn't mean that I need to read the Bible constantly and seclude myself from interactions with the world. It doesn't mandate that I become a monk and devote every waking moment to the study of God's word. A meditation is simply "the act or process of spending time in quiet thought: an expression of a person's thoughts on something" (Merriam-Webster Online Dictionary). Meditation is both spending time in quiet thought and an expression.

It had long been rumored that men think about sex every seven minutes or so. This was based on data obtained by flawed methodology. Recently, Dr. Terri D. Fisher, Professor of Psychology at The Ohio State University at Mansfield, and colleagues performed a more reliable (e.g., with fewer flaws or limitations) study on this topic using men ages 18-25 years. They found that typically men in their sample thought about sex once or twice an hour. Statistically, this was no more and no less frequent than they were thinking about eating or sleeping. It is not surprising that men think frequently about these basic requirements. The thoughts are innately prevalent because they are required for perpetuation of a species. Psychologists in the past referred to certain of these behaviors as primitive instincts.

> *The Spirit of God's habitation within a man earmarks that man for greatness and for blessing.*

Instincts are innate complex patterns of behavior that exist in most members of a species. Any behavior is instinctive if it is performed without being based upon prior experience or observation It is therefore an expression of innate biological factors. For example, sea turtles are hatched on a beach, but will automatically move toward the ocean without being told to or without having had a prior demonstration of this behavior. A kangaroo climbs into its mother's pouch upon being born, without prior instruction. These are complex patterns of behavior that occur naturally. They are distinguished from reflexes, which are simple uncontrollable responses to a specific stimulus. Most of us easily recognize reflexes like the contraction of the pupil in response to bright light or the jerking movement of the lower leg when the knee is tapped during a doctor's exam.

Reflexes are thus fixed action patterns that cannot be controlled.

Animals do not possess volitional capacity strong enough to disengage from any fixed action pattern, whether simple or complex. Once engaged, a fixed action pattern proceeds unencumbered. In contrast, humans can modify a stimulated fixed action pattern by first consciously recognizing the point of its activation, and then they can volitionally stop doing it. If the action pattern can be overridden, it is not considered an instinct, but rather a drive. Thus, we cannot rely on the age-old excuse that this is the way I was created. In actuality, you were created with the ability to overcome the drive or desires of the flesh by resisting the stimuli that excite the drive. The sequence is stimulus followed by drive followed by action. While the drive remains in us, it is only activated by a stimulus which is usually external in origin. Consequently, the presentation of a stimulus can be modulated, avoided or removed. Once the stimulus activates a drive, the drive produces an action. If the goal is to prevent an action, it can be accomplished by squelching the drive and/or by removing the stimulus.

Our society offers a bombardment of stimuli that engage a drive to produce a subsequent related action. The stimuli exist in things we see and hear. The stimuli are also based on past experiences. A visual or auditory stimulus evokes a recollection of a past experience, and if pleasurable, it induces a behavior that seeks reproduction of the physical stimulus. That sounds complex, but in reality, it isn't. In fact, it's a technique that is commonly used to sell products. The goal of any marketer is to get a consumer to purchase product. To entice consumption of the product or service, the advertiser presents the product in a way that incites a recollection or promise of a pleasurable experience. Whether it's the consumption of a juicy burger or the alluring touch of a female, advertisers know how to appeal to the "drive" of a man, and they do it well. When I refer to advertisers, I'm including anyone or any group of individuals that seek your attention. This includes movies, television shows, print media, music and many other sources. Tremendous research is devoted to understanding what drives human behavior. These tactics are employed to elicit a certain action from the consumer. If we are not conscious to recognize the stimulus, we succumb to the drive and repeatedly produce the action that often (for the believer) is undesired.

> *"... I am of the flesh, sold under sin. For I do not understand my own actions... For I do not do the good I want, but the evil I do not want is what I keep on doing. Now, if I do what I do not want,*

it is no longer I who do it, but sin that dwells within me" (Rom. 7:14-20).

In this passage, Paul sounds utterly conflicted. He says that for some reason he keeps doing the things he doesn't want to do, and the things that he actually wants to do, he can't seem to do. Does that sound familiar? Perplexed, he cries out, *"Who will deliver me...?"* (vs. 24) Who will set me free? He concludes in the following chapter that *"... the law of the Spirit of life has set you free in Christ Jesus from the law of sin and death"* (Rom. 8:2). Those who live according to the flesh will set their minds on the things of the flesh, but those who live according to the Spirit set their minds on the things of the Spirit (vs. 5). The mind that is set on the flesh is hostile to God and cannot submit to God's law. Consequently, those who are in the flesh cannot please God (vs. 7-8). This is why meditation on the word of God is crucially important.

We spend an inordinate amount of time throughout each day meditating on things of the world. Whether it be sex, food or sleep, as suggested in the aforementioned study, or whether it be on obtaining wealth, power or some other goal, our minds are constantly infused with societal influences. It occurs without our knowledge, and if we don't consciously combat the infusion, we become a product of or influenced by the infusion. Have you ever learned the lyrics of a song without intentionally trying to learn them? Through simple repeated exposures to the song, the lyrics are infused into your thoughts and consciousness. Soon, without consciously thinking about it, you start singing the lyrics of the song. This is a meditation. What initially started as a quiet thought subsequently becomes the expression of the thought – a meditation. This is why it is important to cautiously guard the information that is infused.

Personally, I am very selective in my choice of music. This is in part because I am a singer and am aware of how music impacts me. The other reason is because I understand the importance of music as an instrument to influence behavior. Lucifer, prior to being expelled from heaven, was the chief musician of heaven. His body literally produced music that was intended to be used in worship to God. However, his beauty and talent induced him to aspire to replace God, which resulted in his expulsion from heaven. To my knowledge, the Bible does not indicate that he lost any of his musical influence. It therefore stands to reason that he would be most influential in the realm of music. It is evident in the debauchery inspired by the lyrics of many popular songs played on the radio today. But I digress.

Music is often used in the classroom to facilitate learning. Somehow rhythmic and melodious patterns allow neuronal pathways of the brain to be receptive to new information and programming. Most of us learned the alphabet or the months of the year by affiliating it with a melody. Many of the most effective teachers have employed the use of rhythms and melodies to stimulate learning. I believe that these musical patterns are to some extent hypnotic. Now some might view this as an extreme position, but understand that I'm not referring to hypnotism in the sense that you are put in a trance as is seen in bad magic shows that when you awaken from the trance you are under the spell of the hypnotist who commands you to bark like a dog or waddle like a duck. Rather, hypnosis is a state of human consciousness involving focused attention and reduced awareness of the surrounding environment. In this state there is an enhanced capacity for response to suggestion. One of the first things that capture our attention with a song is the instrumental music and rhythm. If these are captivating, it increases our capacity to receive the lyrics (or suggestion) of the song. Music provides the access for the lyrics to stimulate a drive which proceeds to a predictable action. It might be over-reaching to simply suggest that a song will cause a man to perform a certain action. This is not my assertion. I do, however, believe that repeated exposure to the stimulus of a drive eventually predisposes an individual to act on that drive. The only way to avoid the natural progression from stimulus to drive to action is to consciously interrupt the process. Without this conscious effort, we proceed to the action that naturally follows.

The Bible says, *"Faith comes from hearing, and hearing through the word of Christ"* (Rom. 12:17). Faith then produces an action, if it is to exist. Biblical proof states, *"Faith by itself, if it does not have works, is dead"* (Jas. 2:17). In this regard, faith is a "drive" that produces an action. It *"is the substance of things hoped for, the evidence of things not seen"* (Heb. 11:1, KJV). Faith, a spiritual drive, is fed by the word of God that we hear. But if it doesn't manifest its associated action, it dies. Similarly, our carnal drives are fed by stimuli that we encounter through our hearing and/or our sight. The lifeline of a drive is its stimulus and its expression. When drives are denied, they die. Thus, we have the ability to kill an unhealthy drive by consciously depriving it of stimulus or by denying its expression as an action.

Crucifying the flesh has been a long-misunderstood concept, particularly amongst Christians who are young in their faith. I can see how this can be confusing. Crucifixion is what we understand that Christ endured as a penance for our sins. No one wants to suffer what Christ went through, and we certainly wouldn't elect to do this to ourselves.

Crucifixion was a humiliating and cruel method of execution by which people were individually hanged, usually by their arms, from a cross or similar structure until they died. It was used in many parts of the world throughout many time periods. It was perhaps best-known as a method used in the Roman Empire about 2000 years ago as means of inducing social control and punishment. The actual mechanism of death caused by crucifixion has perplexed the medical field. It has been proposed that the actual cause of death was dehydration, suffocation, blood loss, fat embolism and various other potential lethal events (J R Soc Med. 2006 Apr; 99(4): 185–188).

The lifeline of a drive is its stimulus and its expression. When drives are denied, they die.

It is also proposed that there were psychological influences that contributed to the death of the one being crucified. While it is not clearly known which of these actually induces the death (which likely varies depending on the method of crucifixion), I think it is reasonable to state that death by crucifixion occurs by denying the body what it needs to survive. Whether it is food, water, oxygen, blood or dignity, crucifixion deprived the body of each. With time, the body suffered, and death was inevitable. As previously mentioned, a drive requires a stimulus and expression to survive or to thrive. Crucifying the flesh simply involves denying the flesh (or the drive) what it needs to survive and thrive – stimulus and expression.

When a man worships, his mind is fixed on God. He meditates on the word of God and secures his gates of influences (e.g., his eyes and his ears) to prevent the infusion of stimuli that feed his unhealthy drives. He takes command of his body and refuses to allow the whims of his unhealthy drives to be expressed. He identifies the stimuli that feed the drive and is cautious to avoid indulgence of the stimuli. Instead, he selectively infuses his mind with godly thoughts and desires. The Bible confirms this by stating, *"Whatsoever things are true, whatsoever things are honest, whatsoever things are just, whatsoever things are pure, whatsoever things are lovely, whatsoever things are of good report; if there be any virtue, and if there be any praise,"* [*a man who worships* will] think on these things (Phil. 4:8). God and his word then become the stimulus for his drive (faith) to live a righteous life (action). In taking his thoughts captive, he can become free at last

NEW LIFE

"You gave me new life; now I'm living again. No longer my life, but it's yours, my friend."

"Therefore, if anyone is in Christ, he is a new creation. The old has passed away; behold, the new has come" (2 Cor. 5:17).

There is perhaps no more liberating scripture in the Bible than 2 Corinthians 5:17. It is assuring to know that all the things that we did in our past can instantly be eradicated and have no relevance to our future. When "the new" comes, the old is rendered completely irrelevant and feckless. However, becoming a whole new creation is difficult to conceptualize. In part, because when we look at our hands and feet, they look the same as they did before the moment we accepted Christ. Our voice sounds the same, and everyone who sees us still recognizes us as the people we were three days before. What may be even more distressing is the finding that we still have some of the same desires, temptations or urges that we had before the moment of our salvation. So, what's new?

The newness is evidenced by a consciousness of our sin and how it separates us from God. This consciousness induces a discontent for allowing the sin of our past to persist where it can plague our present and future. Acceptance of salvation through Christ Jesus opens the door for our relationship and communion with God to be restored. In a previous chapter, we mentioned how a stimulus provokes a drive, and the drive induces an action. If acceptance of salvation is the action, then the drive that compels the action is faith. Hearing the gospel of love is then the stimulus that provoked the drive (faith). The passage from Romans 10 gives somewhat of a visual:

"For whosever shall call upon the name of the Lord shall be saved. How then shall they call [action] on him in whom they have not believed? And how shall they believe [drive] in him of whom they have not heard? And how shall they hear [stimulus] without a preacher?" (vs. 13-14)

In this passage of scripture, we see how the stimulus-drive-action sequence is activated. Someone shared with you the good news of Christ's love. That stimulus provoked a drive of faith and a longing to commune with God, which in turn, induced the action of surrender. While this was effective to draw you to Christ, the work was not finished in the act of surrender. Rather, the work merely began at that time. In Romans 12, Paul beseeches each of us, by the mercies of God, to present our bodies a living sacrifice, holy and acceptable unto God (vs. 1) He continues saying, *"Do not be conformed to this world, but be transformed by the renewal of your mind, that by testing you may discern what is the will of God, what is good and acceptable and perfect"* (vs. 2). There is a lot to unpack in these two, simple and frequently quoted Bible verses.

What does it mean to present our bodies as a living sacrifice? Let's first recall that in the Old Testament, animals were slaughtered and presented on the altar before God as a sacrifice to atone for the sins of mankind. Obviously, Paul is not suggesting that we kill ourselves and offer our dead carcasses as a sacrifice. Rather, he is suggesting that we crucify our flesh. Crucifixion produced death by starving the body of the nutrients and substances needed for survival. When we crucify the flesh, we deny the body the satisfaction of fulfilling its every desire or innate drives. The more we feed or gratify our carnal desires, the stronger they become. However, when we deny the flesh of the fulfillment it requires for life, it dies and becomes less influential in our lives.

The astute biblical scholar will remind me that the animal offered to God in the Old Testament was to be without blemish. It was supposed to be spotless. How, then can we present our bodies in such a fashion when we have sinned and continue to sin – especially as a new Christian? When we accept Christ as our savior, we understand that we continue to get washed of our blemishes each time we ask forgiveness in the name of Jesus. John illustrates this idea for us:

"If we say that we have no sin, we deceive ourselves, and the truth is not in us. If we confess our sins, he [God] is faithful and just to forgive us our sins, and to cleanse us from all unrighteousness" (I John 1:8-9).

To clarify, confession of our sins and the forgiveness obtained through the blood of Jesus makes us spotless in the sight of God. At that moment, we are able to present our bodies before God, holy and acceptable. No matter how great the sin that we committed was, it is washed completely away – *"as far as the east is from the west, so far does he remove our transgressions from us"* (Ps. 103:12). We no longer have to feel guilt or shame because of the sin. In fact, we are then permitted access to commune with God, and it does not depend on another person's assessment of our worthiness for such a privilege. Because we continue to live and interact in this fallen world, there will come another occasion for sin. Just as before, in that circumstance, we acknowledge our sin, ask for forgiveness and are cleansed again. In so doing, we become living sacrifices offered unto God because we live but repeatedly offer our bodies (e.g., will, passions and desires) as sacrifices. He then uses our surrendered bodies however He chooses to use them.

Paul makes it clear that the sanctification and offering of our bodies and our wills can only be accomplished by the mercies of God. Moreover, we don't deserve to be made clean. But, it's by God's mercies that we are able to be cleansed and presented before the Lord, holy and acceptable for His use. We can't will ourselves to holiness. It is only accomplished by the unfailing love of God. In Jeremiah 31:3, the Lord declared to his people: *"I have loved you with an everlasting love; therefore I have continued my faithfulness to you."* At the time of Christ, God affirmed and demonstrated His love in offering his Son to be the ultimate sacrifice whereby we can be cleansed from our unrighteousness. Today, His love and His mercy remain unchanged, thus allowing us a continuous mechanism for being reunited with God.

---

*Acceptance of salvation through Christ
Jesus opens the door for our
relationship and communion with God
to be restored.*

Clearly, living holy before the Lord is a "process." It is not a single magical "poof," and then you're holy for the rest of your life. Paul admonishes us to not be conformed to this world but instead to be transformed. Transformation is the process, and it occurs only with the ongoing renewal of your mind. You've spent most of your life thinking a certain way. Perhaps it was a mindset like many of us who say, "Nobody tells me what to do; I'm a grown man." Some of us have the mindset that I can do it all on my own and don't need anybody's help. Others might believe that there are no redeemable qualities in them. Regardless of the mindset, that sound bite has been playing repeatedly in your mind for years or decades. It is not like a musical device that you can turn on or off – up or down. These are ideals that have shaped who you have become. Like a stream of water that flows through a mountain side and carves its path, our thoughts carve the path for our present and future. Mark 7 reminds us to monitor our thoughts:

"What comes out of a person is what defiles him. For from within, out of the heart of man, come evil thoughts, sexual immorality, theft, murder, adultery, coveting, wickedness, deceit, sensuality, envy, slander, pride, foolishness. All these evil things come from within, and they defile a person" (vs. 20-23).

If left unchecked, our thoughts will destroy us from the inside out. There is a great fallacy in believing that as long as we think it but don't act on the thoughts, then no harm is done. In reality, our thoughts are merely predecessors to actions. Unless they are brought into subjectivity, they will eventually manifest the associated action. Moreover, God knows everything about us and discerns our thoughts from afar (Ps. 139:1-2). Because He knows our end, He sees the path that our thoughts are forging for our lives. Knowing this and its impact on His plans and purposes for us, God urges us to *"Keep thy heart with all diligence; for out of it are the issues of life"* (Prov. 4:23, KJV).

Grace is a divine empowerment by God to do a thing that we are unable to do on our own.

To renew our minds, we practice the admonishment of Paul: *"Let this mind be in you, which was also in Christ Jesus"* (Phil. 2:5, KJV). The mind of Christ was such that even though He knew He was God, He made himself of no reputation but rather took on the form of a servant. He humbled himself and became obedient even unto the death of the cross (Phil. 2:7-8). When we humble ourselves and become obedient to God, He begins to renew our minds which allows the transformative work of the cross to take effect in our lives. This requires that we first recognize and accept that there is no innately good thing that the natural body desires. In fact, it is at constant war with the spirit. Romans 8 is a reminder of that: *"For the mind that is set on the flesh is hostile to God, for it does not submit to God's law; indeed, it cannot"* (vs. 7). When thoughts contrary to the word or will of God arise, we should demolish them just as 2 Corinthians 10 says: *"We destroy arguments and every lofty opinion raised against the knowledge of God, and take every thought captive to obey Christ..."* (vs. 5). I recognize that it is not easy to conquer the recitative voice of the past or even the present, but with continual feeding of the mind with godly thoughts, the mind can and will be renewed. When thoughts of the old man creep up, we must take command of those thoughts and counter them with things that are true, honest, just, pure, lovely and of good report (Phil. 4:8). When the mind continues to wander, we should make sure that we commit our work to the Lord. He will then establish our thoughts (Prov. 16:3), and the "the new" will follow.

Renewal of the mind is not easily accomplished, but God is faithful to provide grace that is sufficient to help us. Grace has frequently been defined as God's unmerited favor in our lives. While it is true that we don't deserve his favor, grace is so much more than this. Grace is a divine empowerment by God to do a thing that we are unable to do on our own. Three times Paul begged the Lord to remove whatever temptation or thought he had; each time to no avail. It might not seem like a lot to us to ask God three times for something and it still not have manifested. Perhaps that's a testimony to how weak our faith is in comparison to Paul's. Paul was so confident that if he asked God for something, God would be faithful to provide it. However, in this circumstance, God still hadn't performed the thing after Paul asked a whopping three times. To Paul, that was apparently excessive, and he resolved to the notion that it was not going to be done. He likely accepted that he was asking the wrong thing of God which was confirmed in God's reply, *"My grace is sufficient for you..."* (2 Cor. 12:9). Rather than contend with God and His will, Paul resigned to the idea that this weakness he had would not be removed. He revised his request from having the "thorn" in his flesh eradicated to allowing God's grace to cover that drive so that it never manifests as an action.

Our thoughts carve the path for our present and future.

To better understand grace, I use the analogy of a sock. The first thing we should acknowledge is that there is nothing that this flesh is incapable of doing if given the right set of circumstances. Yes, the good doctor is capable of stealing, lying, cheating, murder, adultery, homosexuality and drug abuse. It is not a character flaw; rather, it is the nature of the flesh. Romans 3:10 tells us that there is no one who is righteous but God. Lest you boast that some of your good deeds make you righteous, remember Isaiah 64:6 tells us that all of our righteousness is as filthy rags in the sight of God. As Jesus humbled himself, we should humble ourselves and acknowledge, "Yes, my flesh is capable of that too." Humility is the prerequisite for God's grace. The Bible clearly states that *"God opposes the proud but gives grace to the humble"* (Jas. 4:6). If we contend that we would not commit any of these or other sins, we disqualify ourselves from God's grace unless we condition our contention with a phrase similar to, "by the grace of God." We acknowledge that it is only by God's grace that we don't fall prey to many of the temptations of the flesh. Like a sock covers exposed sin, grace covers the weakness of our flesh. Where grace is deficient in our lives, that area of our flesh is exposed.

Remember, you and I are capable of performing any sin. For some, lying might be located at a level high on the calf and stealing might be down low by the toe. As the grace begins to slack, more of the flesh is exposed. In this scenario, it would manifest as lying before it shows up as stealing. For another person, stealing might be located at the level of the calf and homosexuality located at the ankle. The commonality for all of us is that we are slaves to the flesh unless the grace of God empowers us to resist the manifestation of the drive. Paul recognized that a part of his flesh was being exposed by this thorn. After accepting that this was not going to change, he learned to "pull his socks up" and let God's grace cover that area of exposed flesh.

Humility is the prerequisite for God's grace.

In his search for a plausible answer, Paul asked a valid question: "*What shall we say then? Shall we continue in sin, that grace may abound? God forbid. How shall we, that are dead to sin, live any longer therein?*" (Rom. 6:1). Paul aptly addressed the concern that the Christians in Rome had in trying to understand how grace worked. Grace is not God's permission to sin. It is his covering of our sinful nature until we have sufficiently mastered our drives and are able to prevent them from manifesting in action. Grace paints a picture on the outside that is better than that which is on the inside, until the inside matches the outside. It is the fond way in which people see you, but only you and God know that you don't yet measure up to that image. God's grace prevents our secret sin from becoming a public embarrassment of us and Him. It would be tempting to be content with hiding our sin or sinful nature because we know that grace is there covering it. But Paul vehemently forbade that mindset.

How can we continue to live in this contentment when we claim to be dead to sin? Instead we have been given grace upon grace (John 1:16) that allows us to privately measure up to the standard that is presented publicly. God provides a level of grace or covering for our sins until we have matured to the point where we are not easily influenced by that drive. Because of grace, no one knows that the drive is a thorn in your flesh but you and God. As you crucify the flesh, that drive becomes less influential over your thoughts and actions. Let's say for example, it moves from the calf to the level of the ankle. Therefore, you're not as easily susceptible to stimuli that would provoke that drive to manifest as action. At this point, God provides a new level of grace that allows you to conquer another drive at a different level. When that drive is crucified, He provides grace to address yet another drive. Eventually, even the small "foxes" in your life that would otherwise ruin the vine will be eliminated. By repeating this process, you sanctify your body and become a new creation, ready and acceptable for use by God.

Like a sock covers exposed sin, grace covers the weakness of our flesh.

When the new comes, it may be difficult for those who knew you previously to see the new. As you are aware, you still have the same physical attributes that you did before salvation. It might take time for friends and relatives to see you in a different light. But it will happen. Continue walking in the faith and with the mind renewal that causes transformation. Lazarus was in the grave for three days before Jesus arrived. Before his death, his sisters had faith to believe that he could be healed. However, Jesus seemed to delay in getting to address the needs of Lazarus and his sisters. Consequently, he died. After three days, Jesus arrived and declared, *"I am the resurrection, and the life: he that believeth in me, though he were dead, yet shall he live"* (John 11:25). He commanded Lazarus to come forth.

"And he that was dead came forth, bound hand and foot with graveclothes: and his face was bound about with a napkin. Jesus Saith unto them, loose him, and let him go" (vs. 44).

Loose him, and let him go! These words were as powerful as his commandment for Lazarus to come forth. It demonstrates that even after a revival, more work is needed to completely walk in the new life. Jesus could easily have had Lazarus come forth, already freed from the graveclothes. In fact, when Jesus was resurrected, His graveclothes remained in the tomb. But Lazarus was still bound even though he was resurrected. He was bound – hand, foot and face – with the graveclothes. To me, that suggests that even though we have been redeemed, our hands still want to perform some of the actions that the old man desired. Our feet still may want to go the places the old man went. And, when others view us, they might not fully see the change until the full transformative work is complete.

I believe that when we have genuine communion with God, it literally changes how people see us. When Moses returned from communing with God in the tent, there was a glow about his face that was noticed by the people (Exod. 34:29-30). I am not suggesting that we should have a halo around our faces or heads to suggest that we've been with God. But it should be evident when someone has an inward peace that is brought about by worshiping and communing with God. We should strive to live a life that is so constantly surrendered to God that we commune with him on a constant basis, just as Adam walked and talked with God in Eden, before sin.

Loose him, and let him go!

The newness of life brought about by acceptance of salvation in Jesus Christ is an ongoing process that involves that gradual transformation and renewing of the mind. When we accept Christ, we should no longer feel condemned by the sins of our past. Though we might still be tempted with the things from our old life, we now have a consciousness of sin that prevents us from being content living in that sin. There is an inward compulsion that drives us to do the work of transformation. Just as we do not condemn ourselves for the sins of the past, we also don't beat ourselves up for still struggling with some of the drives that motivated us previously. Instead, by humbling ourselves and acknowledging that there is nothing righteous about the flesh, we make ourselves eligible for the grace of God that allows us to overcome those temptation. We submit ourselves unto God and resist the devil, knowing that when we do this, he will flee from us (Jas. 4:7). With an ongoing commitment to crucifying the flesh and with the empowerment of God's grace, the new life is given expression *when a man worships*.

I'M RUNNING

*"Right now, I'm ready. Right now, I'm willing.
Wherever you lead me, I'm running for you."*

*"... Let us also lay aside every weight, and sin which
clings so closely, and let us run with endurance the
race that is set before us" (Heb. 12:1).*

The renewing of our minds and the transformation of our beings are a continual process. In fact, it is a lifelong process. There's a modification of an old Chinese proverb that says the journey of a thousand miles begins with a single step. Even the longest and most difficult ventures have a starting point. That's where we start in our walk with Christ – the first step. The first step is the acceptance of Christ as Lord and Savior. We then continue with the transformation of our minds, wills and desires. With a renewed mind and a transformed body, we mature toward use in service by the Lord. Worship is instrumental throughout the process – from the initial step of salvation, to the continual use in God's service and until our lives end. Paul, in the final days of his life of ministry, told Timothy, *"I have fought the good fight, I have finished the race, I have kept the faith. Henceforth there is laid up for me the crown of righteousness, which the Lord, the righteous judge, will award to me on that day..."* (2 Tim. 4:7-8). He understood the necessity and reward of being steadfast in his devotion, worship and service to God.

One of my favorite passages of scripture that illustrates the "process" of worship is Isaiah 6. In this passage, the prophet has a unique and magnificent encounter with God. He had a vision of the Lord sitting on the throne, in all of His glory. Before Him were majestic creatures, angels, that themselves were overwhelmed by the glory that emitted from God. Overtaken by God's glory, the angels covered their faces and their feet. The angels flew around the throne and called one to another, "Holy, holy, holy is the Lord of hosts; the whole earth is full of his glory!" (vs. 3). When the Lord spoke, the foundations of the earth shook, and the house filled with an awesome cloud of smoke. Recognizing that he was in the presence of pure holiness, the prophet cried out, *"Woe is me! For I am lost; for I am a man of unclean lips and I dwell in the midst of a*

*people of unclean lips; for my eyes have seen the King,
the Lord of hosts!"* (vs. 5).

This is what happens when we draw close to God.
The light of His glory shines on us, and we begin to see
ourselves as we really are. There is no hiding or
disguising our uncleanness. I am convinced that many of
us have never genuinely encountered the glory of God.
Certainly, if we could be content about our unrighteous
state, we are not spending enough time (or any time)
before His throne in worship. Worship reveals what's in
us. In worship, hidden sins are brought to light not for
the purpose of condemnation, but for the purpose of
sanctification.

In Isaiah 6, after the prophet recognized his unclean
state, angels were immediately dispensed to him. They
placed a burning coal from the altar on his mouth. With
this, his guilt was purged, and his sins were atoned. God
then asked, *"Whom shall I send, and who will go for us?"*
After his purging, Isaiah was able to answer the Lord
saying, *"Here I am! Send me"* (vs. 8). In this passage,
we see the dynamic of worship. Isaiah had an intimate
encounter in the presence of God. In the light of God's
glory, Isaiah's uncleanness was revealed. He was then
purged and made ready for God's use. Worship prepares
a man to be used by God.

When a man worships, just like Isaiah, he is cleansed
and subsequently charged by God to do a work that he

otherwise would be unequipped and incapable of doing. In a sense, it's like the runners in a track meet. They hear the call, "On your mark, get set, go!" On your mark means to be in the at the right place at the right time. Getting set means that you assume the proper position to be effective and victorious. Then, you're ready to go! However, this race is not a sprint – it's a marathon. It's a lifelong race; pace yourself.

The newness of salvation is invigorating. The discovery that God loves us enough in our sinful state to allow a path for our freedom from the bondage of sin is alone thrilling. Add to that the knowledge that He will not hold our past sins against us, and we are free to start afresh.

Who couldn't be excited about getting out and sharing that Good News? Motivated by our newfound liberty, we are anxious to get out in the field and start harvesting souls. So, we start with a sprint. We eagerly do all that we can to express our gratitude for the gift of life that has been given to us. While this enthusiasm is laudable, we must have the endurance to finish the race, and this can only be accomplished with continual learning and soberness of mind. The worst that could happen is that in our zeal to preach the kingdom of God, we lose steam, become fatigued by the burden of the call and eventually turn away. The Bible tells us that the man who puts his hands to the plow and turns back is unfit for the kingdom of God (Luke 9:62). That means, when we start the race – you and I must finish it.

In worship, hidden sins are brought to light not for the purpose of condemnation, but for the purpose of sanctification.

If you've ever participated in a race, you'll understand that before you can get on your mark, you must be registered for the race. For many races, there is a registration fee. There is a cost to running this race of salvation and service to God. When Jesus called His disciples, there was one who said to Him, *"I will follow you wherever you go"* (Luke 9:57), but he didn't realize following Jesus meant potentially having no established home or place to lay his head. To another Jesus said, "Follow me." The man replied, "First let me go bury my father." Burying a parent was perhaps the ultimate sign of respect and honor to a parent in his culture. Still, Jesus told him, *"Leave the dead to bury their own dead. But as for you, go and proclaim the kingdom of God"* (vs. 60). This race requires that you count the costs before getting on the mark. Perhaps for you it might mean that you abandon your dreams of owning a big house or stylish car. Perhaps it means that you need to forsake some of your cultural norms and family traditions – even

91

at the risk of being criticized by those who are close to you. Jesus gave some hard words to people who wanted to be his disciples:

> *"If anyone comes to me and does not hate his own father and mother and wife and children and brothers and sisters, yes, and even his own life, he cannot be my disciple...For which of you, desiring to build a tower, does not first sit down and count the cost, whether he has enough to complete it?"* *(Luke 14:26-28).*

Ouch! Is Jesus requiring that you hate your relatives and your own life? I don't believe He literally intends for you to hate them. However, He unquestionably means that if you love them more than you love Him, you cannot do what is required to be His disciple. This is the registration fee that you and I must consider or the cost we should count before committing to run this race of faith.

Once we have counted the cost, we get on our marks – be in the right place at the right time with the expectation to run and win. This means that the places we used to go, we might not be able to go anymore. In 2 Corinthians 6:14, Paul asks a very vital question: *"... what partnership has righteousness with lawlessness? Or what fellowship has light with darkness?"* Have you ever asked yourself, "What am I doing here?" When you have been redeemed from a life of sin and separation from God and then try to hang with some of the same crowd or in some of the same places you did previously, you quickly realize that you no longer belong there. It's like trying on a pair of shoes that your feet have outgrown. You might still like the shoes and have fond memories of when you wore them, but they just don't fit anymore. In fact, when you try to force your foot into them, you experience more pain than it is worth simply for the satisfaction of having fit into them. So is the case when we try to put the new man back into the old man's environment and role. The scriptures warn us that this is an unwise practice: *"no one puts new wine into old wineskins. If he does, the wine will burst the skins—and the wine is destroyed, and so are the skins"* (Mark 2:22).

When I lived in a very urban part of Cincinnati, called Over the Rhine, I was trying hard to live a righteous life. There was a night club that was about two blocks away from my home. Every Saturday night, if I would ride past it, I would see a long line of people waiting to get into the joint. I had lived there for more than three years and never set foot in the club. One night, I determined that I would be adventurous and go inside. I wasn't in there fifteen minutes before something in me said, "You don't belong here." Not long afterward, I heard the firing of gun shots.

At the time, I was working as a funeral director/embalmer and immediately recalled a professional football player that I embalmed. This gentleman had just started playing for the Indianapolis Colts and was positioned for an excellent future as a professional athlete. One night at a different club, he became the unintended victim of gunfire and died. That Saturday night as I lay on the ground, I realized that just like that professional athlete, I could be at the wrong place at the wrong time, and my God ordained purpose could be snatched from me in a moment's notice. While this could happen any place, there are some decisions that I could make to ensure that if my time clock expired too soon, it was not because I was in a place or "wearing a garment" that no longer fits me. Obviously, I was delivered from that situation without injury, but with a very valuable lesson – to be mindful about always being on my mark, in the right place and at the time I am supposed to be.

We each have an appointment with destiny and an appointed time to receive the blessing of God. But we have to be properly positioned to receive it. At the appointed time, God told Elijah to get up from the brook where he was being constantly fed by God during a famine. He was told go to Zarephath, where God had already prepared a widowed woman to feed him. Keep in mind, this woman had no money and barely had enough meal left to bake bread so that she and her son

94

could eat their last meal and die of starvation. Elijah obeyed,

> *"so, he arose and went to Zarephath. And when he came to the gate of the city, behold, a widow was there gathering sticks. And he called to her and said, 'Bring me a little water in a vessel, that I may drink'" (I Kings 17:10).*

The widow could easily go get the water, but Elijah also asked her for a morsel of bread. Being stretched beyond the capacity she felt she had, she proceeded to explain her desperate situation to the prophet. Nonetheless, he didn't relent in his request, knowing God had promised that the woman's *"jar of flour shall not be spent, and the jug of oil shall not be empty, until the day that the Lord sends rain upon the earth"* (vs. 14). The woman went and did as Elijah commanded. As a result of her obedience, she and her household ate for many days, and indeed the jar of flour was not spent, neither did the jug of oil become empty, just as God had promised Elijah. All this happened because the woman was where God had appointed her to be when she encountered the prophet.

The Bible says the widow was gathering sticks when Elijah came. Gathering sticks seem to be such an insignificant activity to initiate such a weighty encounter

95

with God. We often expect that God needs to part the heavens and have angels descend in melodic chorus for us to receive the blessing from God. However, God's appointments are often synchronous with the mundane activities that we do in our daily lives. God does not, or should not, need to only reveal Himself to us when we are immersed in the expert performance of an anointed worship team in corporate worship. During corporate worship we are only better able to hear God because the corporate environment forces us to focus on God and to listen for His voice during those times. However, when we practice daily communion with God, He speaks just as clearly during the routine of our day. David was ordained king by Samuel while he was tending sheep. This widow received the blessing of her life while simply gathering sticks, preparing to die from starvation with her son. So, don't be disappointed when it seems that things aren't working out as you had hoped they would, and it seems that you have been forsaken. Don't think that you must do some extravagant stunt to garner God's attention and intervention.

Worship prepares a man to be used by God.

Keep the faith. Go and do what God commands because you never know when your Elijah will be presented to you and will prophesy that your barrels won't go empty. Therefore, *"... let us not be weary in well doing: for in due season we shall reap, if we faint not"* (Galatians 6:9). This widow was exactly where God intended her to be before He intervened. She was on her mark, and she was also set. She received the instruction of God's prophet and positioned herself to receive the blessing by her obedience. Her last step was to go – go and prepare the morsel of bread that was requested by the prophet and ordained by God.

Like the widow, we must be positioned and prepared to be used by God. Preparation for God's race has one qualifying criteria – that is submission. Submission to the sovereignty of God is a key ingredient of worship and positions us for use in service to God. The recognition that God is greater than we are allows us to surrender to His guidance and commands. He provides an assignment to each of us as we go along this journey. While the revelation of the assignment might be news to you, it was known by God before the foundation of the world. God told Jeremiah, *"Before I formed you in the womb I knew you, and before you were born I consecrated you; I appointed you a prophet to the nations"* (Jer. 1:5).

This is reassuring because it means that before we had our DNA constitution, God knew the plan that He had for us. The blueprint was already drawn before the materials list was created. God, being a masterful

97

creator, doesn't wait to see what He created only later to determine what its purpose will be. He doesn't try to force-fit the creation to meet a purpose. He knows the purpose and forms the creation to meet the purpose. Because He knew what He desired of you before He formed you, He had clear instructions of what would be required to accomplish that goal. So, your eye color, body habitus, height, personality, tone of your voice, etc. were all masterfully designed to fulfill the purpose He has for you. He also knew what your passions, dislikes and capacity would be and created them to suit the purpose He envisioned for you. So, there is no sense in allowing any of your physical, intellectual or temperamental attributes to dissuade you from the purpose God created for you.

The story of David and Goliath demonstrates the assurance of God's creation and preparation. Although he was of small stature and young in age, David knew that what God created in him was sufficient to slay the giant, Goliath. However, others including King Saul and David's own brothers had no confidence that he could defeat the giant. King Saul said to David, *"You are not able to go against this Philistine to fight with him for you are but a youth, and he has been a man of war from his youth"* (I Sam. 17:33). But David recounted for Saul how when a lion or a bear would come and take one of his father's lambs, David would fight and kill them. He confidently said, *"Your servant has struck down both lions and bears, and this uncircumcised Philistine shall be like one of them..."* (vs. 36). Notice he said "lions and bears," meaning more than one lion and more than one bear. David had history with God. With each victory, his trust in God grew stronger and stronger.

At this point, David was confident that God was for him, and consequently, no one could be against him, especially not one who had defied the armies of the living God. Needless-to-say, David prevailed against the giant. Why? Because David spent time with God and in that time, God affirmed to David who he was and for what purpose he was created. In his time of worship, David became intimately aware of how he was created and for what purpose he existed. As a quintessential worshiper, spending countless hours in communion with God, he understood who he was to God and who God was to him. He discovered that he was fearfully and wonderfully made (Ps. 139:14) and that the righteous would never be forsaken (Ps. 37:25). David knew his calling in Christ. He knew his purpose, but only by seeking God and spending time in communion with him.

When a man worships, he acknowledges his frailties and gets purged of them. In frequent communion with God, he discovers who he is and why he was created. No discouragement from others or from the voices within his head will dissuade him from pursuit of that purpose. He learns his strengths, his weaknesses, his passions and his aversions. His enlightenment helps him maximally utilize these attributes to fulfill the purpose for which God created him. With each new victory and by proving the promises of God, he gains confidence knowing that when he sets out on his ordained path, God will faithfully guide and defend him. But, before setting out on the journey, he counts the costs of his commitment. He positions himself to be timely present for a lifelong series of sequential encounters with God that situate him for a successful race. To the man who worships, the benefit of perpetual communion with God is all that matters and is worth any sacrifice he makes. His goal is to remain on his mark and set to go wherever God leads. When his pursuits are rightly aligned with God, *"the heart of a man plans his way, but the Lord establishes his steps"* (Prov. 16:9).

WHEN A MAN
WORSHIPS

*"When a man worships, he'll know how to treat his
woman right."*

*"Husbands, love your wives, as Christ loved the
church and gave himself up for her..." (Eph. 5:25).*

There should be no relationship that better mimics
God's love for his people than that of a husband and
wife. Because marital relationships have been defiled,
people find it hard to receive God's love when it is made
analogous to that of husband. When they see how easily
the marital relationship is annulled, they mistakenly
believe that the love of God is similarly fleeting. If we
are to adequately demonstrate God's love for humans,
we must first master the love that we have for those

whom we see and especially for the one with whom we made a lifelong covenant. Paul instructed men to love their wives as Christ loved the church. To understand what that means and how it is manifested, we much first consider how Christ loved the church and what that love looked like. To illustrate this, we will explore the relationship of Jacob and Rachel.

Remember that Abraham was promised by God to be the father of many nations. Even though he and his wife, Sarah, were old, God promised the two of them a child. I call this the Seed of Promise. Growing weary of waiting, Sarah convinced Abraham to have a child with one of their servants. This was a substitute but not the seed. God intended for a specific blood line for his promise, and Isaac was that chosen seed. In his old age, Abraham and Sarah finally bore Isaac. Isaac took a wife, and with her a Seed of Promise was born, Jacob. Further down the lineage, eventually, the ultimate Seed of Promise, Jesus, was born. But he would not have come if there had been no marriage between Jacob and Rachel.

Jacob met Rachel at a well when he was fleeing from his brother. Apparently, wells were frequent pickup spots in the Bible. It seems that a lot of women got their "Mrs." degree after meeting a man at the well. But that's beside the point – just a casual observation. When Jacob laid eyes on Rachel, he fell in love. The Bible describes

Rachel as *"beautiful in form and appearance"* (Gen. 29:17). Clearly, she was pretty and had an enticing body. She caught the eye, attention and affection of Jacob immediately. He was welcomed into the home of Laban, Rachel's father, and began working for Laban. Laban was committed to paying Jacob a wage for the work he did for him. Instead of collecting a wage, Jacob agreed to work seven years for Laban to have Rachel as his wife. Because Jacob loved Rachel so much, the seven years seemed only like a few days (vs. 20).

At the end of seven years, Jacob was ready to collect and receive Rachel as his bride. Laban threw a big party in celebration of the wedding. Apparently, there must have been a lot of drinking going on because Jacob didn't realize that when he was consummating his marriage, he was doing so with Leah, the older sister, and not Rachel – the one for whom he worked seven years to marry. When he awakened in the morning, he expected to see the beautiful Rachel beside him but much to his disappointment, he saw Leah, the ugly sister. Jacob was livid and confronted Laban. *"Laban said, 'It is not so done in our country, to give the younger before the firstborn"* (vs. 26). Apparently, the custom of the land was that the older sister needed to be married off before the younger, Rachel. Although he was disappointed by this turn of events, Jacob agreed to work another seven years to marry Rachel. The whole time he worked, Jacob remained married to Leah but did not love her – not like he loved Rachel. After another seven years of hard work, he finally married the woman of his dreams, Rachel.

God saw that Leah was hated by Jacob so he decided to make Rachel barren while Leah would bear the children. With each pregnancy, Leah thought for sure Jacob would love her because she bore for him a child. However, his affection was always directed toward Rachel, and Leah felt unloved and unwanted. Even after four children, Jacob's affection never shifted toward Leah. Rachel being angered by her inability to bear children went to Jacob and said, *"Give me children, or I shall die!"* (Gen. 30:1) Jacob replied in similar anger, *"Am I in the place of God, who has withheld from you the fruit of the womb?"* (vs. 2). Like his grandfather and father, Jacob tried to substitute for the Seed of Promise by having children with Rachel's servants, at her suggestion. By the time Rachel's servant bore two children for Jacob, Leah had stopped having children. Instead, she gave her servant to Jacob who bore two more children for him. Jacob was essentially being pimped out by his two wives in a competition to bear his children and compete for his affection. After some bartering with Rachel, Leah slept with Jacob again and started bearing even more children. After the sixth child that she herself bore, Leah thought for sure by now Jacob would honor her. Not so. Despite bearing for him six boys and a daughter, the Bible never says whether

Jacob began to love Leah or not. Eventually, after eleven children were born to Jacob by Leah and the servants of Leah and Rachel, God finally opened Rachel's womb, and she birthed the Seed of Promise, Joseph. Joseph became the favorite child of Jacob because he was born to Rachel, the woman of his dreams. There's probably little surprise why Joseph was despised by his brothers considering his dad hated their mother and put her through years of anguish in trying to acquire his love.

When we refuse to love our spouses, even in their ugliness, they are unable to produce that which God ordained for them to produce.

This seems like a strange story to use in illustration of the idyllic love between a man and his wife. Indulge me for just a moment; I will help it make sense. Let's first consider what initially drew Jacob to Rachel – her outward beauty. It is not clear if she was as beautiful on the inside as she was on the outside, but she was obviously a beauty in the eyes of Jacob. He was willing to work fourteen years just to get her; that says something. She was the woman of his dreams, and he was willing to do whatever it took to fulfill his thirst for her. I can understand that feeling.

I first met Darice, my wife, in the ninth grade. I saw her and told my friend, one day, she will be my wife. While we didn't date in high school, I laid the foundation for my plan, especially in the eleventh and twelfth grades. She would speak more on the telephone with me than she did with her boyfriend. Shortly after we graduated, we dated for a few months before she went away to college. It wasn't long before we knew that the long-distance relationship wouldn't work out so well. Back then, long-distance calls were expensive, and neither of us had money to maintain the relationship. However, I maintained relationship with her mother. I got in good with the mamma – a key strategy. Maybe three years later, Darice moved back home and started attending the University of Cincinnati. I like to believe it was, in large part, to be closer to me. She might deny that, but nonetheless, we stayed in close contact then and during the preceding years when she was away. Now that she had returned to Cincinnati, my opportunity had arrived. A long story short, we eventually started dating and eventually got married. What is my point other than telling you that I'm the man? I don't know.... I just like telling that story.

The reality is, I saw the woman of my dreams and was intent to have her be my wife. I was willing to do whatever it took to make sure she saw me in the same way I saw her, and for six years I pursued (not stalked) her. I wooed her with kindness and friendship. I demonstrated what a respectful love could look like. Even though she had determined that she would never be married, her affection was won by an unbridled but holy pursuit. This is how Christ pursues us. He identifies His church and says I am willing to endure whatever is necessary to have her. She might not initially understand or recognize the beauty of that love, but His persistent pursuit eventually allows her to relent from the shackles of a hurtful past that misrepresents what a healthy relationship can and should look like.

Like Jacob, all my hard work had paid off, and I finally had the woman of my dreams. Until one day, I awakened to the revelation that I thought I was marrying Rachel, but instead I got Leah, the ugly sister. Understand, I am not insulting my wife or calling her ugly. She was a stunningly beautiful woman and today is even more beautiful. I am, however, saying that we all discover some ugliness in our spouse that we did not see before we got married. That happens both ways – with the husband and with the wife. There are habits, mood swings, behaviors and such that we discover and find most distasteful when the newness of the marital bliss wears off. We are now faced with the ugliness of a reality we did not anticipate. I expected rose petals and lilies all the time but overlooked the thorns until they pricked me. This is the point when many of us are tempted to start looking for flowers in another garden, rather than tending our own garden.

Remember in the story, when Jacob discovered that he was stuck with Leah he was angered. Even after getting Rachel, he still hated the ugly sister. Perhaps he despised her because he felt betrayed and tricked into marrying her. She obviously was in on the attempt to deceive Jacob. She knew where his affections were, but she was so intent to be married that she misrepresented who she was. Dating is often a big masquerade. We don't let the person we're dating know who we really are until we have gotten what we want from that person. Eventually, our ugliness is uncovered. When it is unleashed, it reproduces bountifully if it is not appropriately addressed. Leah continued to produce offspring that were birthed from Jacob's refusal to love the ugly sister. All the while, the woman of his dreams remained barren. That barrenness threatened to bring a miserable and untimely death to Rachel's created purpose as suggested by her cry, "Give me a child or else I'll die!"

When we refuse to love our spouses, even in their ugliness, they are unable to produce that which God ordained for them to produce. In fact, they begin to die on the inside as time passes. Jacob was fortunate enough that his wife came to him and begged of him what she needed. We often don't have that luxury, in part because our spouses might not fully know what exactly they need to feel whole or fulfilled. They just realize that there is a hidden creation that they are charged with birthing, but it seems locked up and unable to be released. The key to releasing it is loving the ugly sister in our wives. The more we resist, the more productive the ugly sister becomes. Just like Leah bore seven children out of her discontent with the love she received from her husband, our wives will give birth to offspring that have the potential or at least the motive to destroy the promise that God gave to us. Remember, Jacob had ten children by women other than the woman of his dreams. With Rachel, he had two children, but Joseph was the Seed of Promise. The other eleven despised him and at one point sought to kill him. Nothing will kill the vision of your future faster than a refusal to love your wife even in and through her ugliness. Even our prayers are hindered when we refuse to honor our wives as God intends (I Pet. 3:7). Conversely, when we quickly learn to love the ugly sister, we release the woman of our dreams to be and to produce that which she was created to be and produce.

When we were yet sinners and ugly in all of our ways, Christ died for us (Rom. 5:8). This is how God shows His love for us, and this is how we should demonstrate our love for our wives. The love is not conditioned on her performance of a particular task or adoption of a certain behavior. We love just because! Besides, if we were honest, the things that we dislike in our wives are not new. They didn't just spring up on us overnight. Jacob knew, or should have known, that the custom of the land was that the older sister had to be given in marriage before the younger one could be. He should not have been surprised when this custom was observed. However, he ignored the signs before they got married. Perhaps, he thought things would be different and that the customs of the land did not apply to him. If so, that was obviously wishful thinking. Even if it seemed to work out uncommonly in his favor, how could he not recognize that on the night of his marriage, he was having sex with someone other than the woman of his dreams. I suspect it had something to do with the fact that he had his beer goggles on.

Without inviting a confession, many of the men who will read this book have had a beer goggle encounter. You engaged in a relationship and in hindsight said to yourself (or out loud), "What was I thinking?" We entangle ourselves in relationships that we know are not desirable when we enter them under the influence. Sometimes, that influence is alcohol which may result in a one-night stand. Sometimes there are other influences – loneliness, destitution, horniness, brokenness, anger, rejection. All of these and many other factors influence our ability to see the signs. If we were whole ourselves, those signs would be plainly evident. These revelations would keep us from making a poorly contemplated lifelong covenant. Sometimes, the influence is infatuation or what we call being in love. My encouragement, brothers, is don't be so stricken and starry eyed by love that it impedes your vision. See what is plainly before you. Look beyond the outward beauty; pay attention to the ugly sister who lies deceptively beneath the exterior and patiently waits for you to foolishly enter a relationship that will eventually be toxic.

Don't say "Amen!" too quickly. Once you've made that covenant and realized you got Leah instead of Rachel, there is a remedy other than divorce. Learn to love the ugly sister. As God told Jeremiah, *"...I have loved thee with an everlasting love: therefore with lovingkindness have I drawn thee"* (Jer. 31:3, KJV). We can manifest the woman of our dreams with lovingkindness. The woman of our dreams isn't revealed in all of her glory until we demonstrate the type of love for our wives that God demonstrated for the church. That love is not conditioned on the church's performing rituals, presenting itself beautifully before God or saying the things that God wants to hear. It is as committed when we do the right things as it is when we are in outright rebellion. This is the expectation for how men are to love their wives:

"Husbands, love your wives, as Christ loved the church and gave himself up for her, that he might sanctify her, having cleansed her by the washing of water with the word, so that he might present the church to himself in

splendor, without spot or wrinkle or
any such thing, that she might be holy
and without blemish" (Eph. 5:25).

Let's break this down a little. The first and perhaps most important part of this commandment that Paul gave is to love your wives as Christ loved the church. How did Christ demonstrate that love? By giving himself up for her. This can be a big pill to swallow. You might ask, "Are you saying that I need to be willing to die for my wife?" The answer – possibly so. It certainly demonstrates a great love. John said it best: *"Greater love has no one than this, that someone lay down his life for his friends"* (John 15:13). Being willing to die for your wife is not only chivalrous, but it is also a powerful demonstration of your love for her. If she doesn't believe that you would take a bullet for her, there's something deficient about the way you're loving her. But this is only one aspect of the type of love that lays down its life.

You might confidently and proudly state that you are willing to die for your wife. But how you are willing to live for your wife? Some might say that in the heat of the moment it is easier to make the rash decision to die for your wife. It might be a little harder to do when you have to contemplate what you will endure or suffer while living with your wife. This is especially difficult when the duration of the suffering is not defined aforehand.

We entangle ourselves in relationships that we know are not desirable when we enter them under the influence.

The moment of death was the easy part for Jesus. The difficult part was living through what was to immediately precede the moment of death. Jesus was likely relieved when he could say "it is finished" and bow his head. When the Bible says "that someone lay down his life" it wasn't just talking about the physical death. It is talking about laying down his preferences, his will, his reputation and in the case of Jesus, even His deity. Jesus, *"though he was in the form of God, did not count equality with God a thing to be grasped but emptied himself, by taking the form of a servant, being born in the likeness of men"* (Phil. 2:6-7). The King James Version says that Jesus made himself of no reputation and became obedient even unto death.

Even when questioned by Pilate as whether He was the son of God, Jesus could have easily proclaimed Himself to be King of the Jews, but He remained humble. He could easily have retaliated when men mocked and beat Him, but He knew that He must lay down His life. He knew He had to lay down even His miraculous power which healed so many and even raised one from the dead. He refused to allow His position or

113

stature to interfere with His mission of sacrifice. He understood the benefit of His sacrifice – that He might present to Himself, a glorious church, not having spot or wrinkle. Jesus understood that though the sacrifice might be great, the reward would be greater.

When we love our wives as Christ loved the church, it manifests as a willingness to lay down our pride, our reputations, our prerogatives and even our credit as a sacrifice. Though the sacrifice might be great, we must realize as Jesus did, that we eventually benefit from the sacrifice. Jesus laid down His life expecting a return on his investment – that is that He would inherit a church without spot or blemish. When we lay down our lives for our wives, we become the beneficiaries. This is how we can create the wives of our dreams and free them to be and produce that which God ordained.

God ordained order in the household places the husband as the head of the wife. He gives specific directions for a wife's role:

> *"Wives, submit yourselves unto your own husbands, as unto the Lord. For the husband is the head of the wife, even as Christ is the head of the church: and he is the saviour of the body" (Eph. 5:22-23, KJV).*

Now, I know I just said a bad word (at least to some) – submit. In fact, I probably said two bad words –

114

submit and sacrifice. No one really wants to do either, but they are both necessary for a successful marriage. This same passage of scripture outlines how women are to submit to their husband and how husbands are to sacrifice for their wives. When marriages fail, most often it is due to a failure to submit and/or sacrifice.

Let's first explore what it really means to submit and why it is necessary. Submission is the fervent commitment to the success of a plan or ideal that you initially opposed. As detailed in a later chapter discussion, we more often acquiesce than submit. To acquiesce means that we accept something reluctantly with or without protest. That is a far cry from submission. When one acquiesces, he or she will agree to the plan but not be actively involved in the success of that plan. In fact, he may often secretly wish for or work toward the failure of the plan so he can have the satisfaction of saying, "I told you so." This is not only unproductive for the relationship, but it is extremely harmful. Submission, on the other hand, is a commitment to make sure that the plan works and works well, even though you initially thought that it wouldn't. Submission adopts the mentality that if we succeed, we succeed together. If we fail, we fail together. This is what becoming one flesh means – God's original intent for marital relationship and balance.

When we lay down our lives for our wives, we become the beneficiaries.

God established the marital covenant when He said, "Therefore shall a man leave his father and his mother, and shall cleave unto his wife: and they shall be one flesh. And they were both naked, the man and his wife, and were not ashamed" (Gen. 2:24-25, KJV). When God created man and woman, he pulled woman out of the side of man and intended for them to be one flesh. In becoming one flesh, they were to walk side by side and mutually accountable to each other. Neither of them had any shame or fault. However, after sin entered the world by their mutual sin, God instituted an order for the marital covenant. Because the woman succumbed first to the devil, God said to her, "I will greatly multiply thy sorrow and thy conception; in sorrow thou shalt bring forth children; and thy desire shall be to thy husband, and he shall rule over thee" (Gen. 3:16, KJV). There are three components to this curse of the woman.

First, he said childbirth would be painful for her. The second and third are the subject of many commentaries. He said that the woman's desire shall be to the husband. This is interpreted many different ways. Some believe that it means that she will always desire to be married. Have you ever wondered why women desire marriage so much? The reality is that marriage is not terribly beneficial for women. They are often (not always) the ones who clean the home and cook. They review the homework with the children and take them to soccer practice. They do this after they've worked a full-time job just like the man. And when it's all said and done, the husband looks to her for sexual gratification. There's no wonder why they might be less interested in sex than men – they're tired!

---

*Though the sacrifice might be great,
the reward would be greater.*

More often than not, in a marriage, the husband has the better deal. All he has to do is go to work, come home, eat and if he plays his cards right, get a little love-making. Why then is it that men avoid marriage, but women dream of the day when they will covenant to this sort of indentured servitude? Even though I help out a lot with the cooking and other family chores, I honestly look at how my wife outperforms me at home and wonder why she does it. More perplexing to me is how she can seem to enjoy it. Perhaps it is because there is a genetic propensity to have this desire when you have two "X" chromosomes. By no means, am I implying that this is universal and predestined for all women. Obviously, women are diverse in their passions and pursuits and with shifts in cultural norms, the roles seem to be reversing in many cases. But if there is an innate longing to fill these roles, it is unquestionably more commonly found in women than men. God bless them!

Another interpretation of the woman's desire being toward the man is that her desires are to be subjected to the man's. This interpretation would be more consistent with the third recompense mentioned in the passage of scripture -- "and he shall rule over thee." In the garden, the serpent tempted the woman first with the fruit. The target of temptation is desire. The weakness in Eve was her desire. One might extrapolate that to mean that despite her many strengths, external desire is the weakness of a woman. That desire is often in search of more – more shoes, more purses, more perfumes, etc. Eve had everything she could want in the garden, but she desired the one thing she was told she could not have – the forbidden fruit. Presumably, if Adam had been present, he might have intervened and prevented her from acting on her desire since he was the one initially given the instruction by God. Perhaps he would still have succumbed to her invitation to eat of the forbidden fruit. After all, his weakness was the woman.

Submission is the fervent commitment to the success of a plan or ideal that you initially opposed.

Throughout scripture and history, we see that a man's greatest vulnerability is to the wiles of a woman. It happened to Samson and David, as previously mentioned. It likely has happened to you, just like it has me. Most of us can at some point in our lives recall a stupid decision we made because of our desire for a woman. So, men are already vulnerable to women. Perhaps it is because they were taken from our side, and there's a constant longing to be restored through the presence of a woman. I don't want to speculate much on the reason, but it is certainly a common observation that has persisted throughout time. If there is a way to tame a man, it will be uncovered by a woman. Because a woman is the weakness of a man, God restored the balance of relationship by making woman subject to the man. Unfortunately, for too many years, that subjection has been abused, and women have been treated as inferior to the man. These are two totally different concepts. It does not mean that the man is obliged to denigrate or mistreat the woman. Instead, being subject to the man means that the woman's desires are subjected to him. His goal is to fulfill that desire if it is healthy, holy and timely.

In reality, a woman can get just about anything she desires from her husband. I am not advocating manipulation by a woman. But just as it is genetically unavoidable that a woman desires to be married (in a majority of cases), it is ontologically improbable that a man will continue to resist the enticement of his wife in a loving and committed marriage. It is a man's desire to please his wife. When she presents her desire to him – or subjects that desire to him – he commits to see that it happens because he desires to please her.

Conversely, when a woman fills that desire apart and independent from her husband, it is an offense to him. It is especially offensive if the desire is filled by another individual – especially another man. A man who worships wants to provide for his wife and will not be content with those provisions being supplied by another. You might call it jealousy or pride, but it is not vastly different from the way that God loves us. God is a jealous God and wants no one providing for His people besides Him. He desires to be the one who fulfills our desires. God lovingly illustrates this to us, His children, when He says,

"If you then, who are evil, know how to give good gifts to your children, how much more will your Father who is in heaven give good things to those who ask him!" (Matt. 7:11).

I can hear it already – the strong-willed feminist saying, "I shouldn't have to ask him when I want something." And I would agree with you. You shouldn't have to ask him. Just know that when you don't submit that desire to him, you subvert his godly authority and rob him of the privilege of fulfilling your desire – that which he lives to do.

The target of temptation is desire.

When submitted to God and with an understanding of his God ordained role, a man is compelled to fulfill his priestly authority as the head of his household. He does not lord his headship over his wife oppressively. Rather, he understands that being the head means that he makes the greater sacrifice. Because Jesus is the head of the church, He was obligated to make the greater sacrifice – His life. The virtuous head of any organization or company understands that when there is a sacrifice to be made, it comes from him/her. As a business owner, my first responsibility is to make sure that my employees are paid. If the bootstraps need to be tightened, mine are the first to be tightened. The one caveat that I mentioned is that the head who is virtuous will do this. This is why it is important to make sure that you know those among whom you labor and to avoid being unequally yoked. When (or better yet, before) you marry, remove the beer goggles so you can clearly see who it is with whom you are entering a lifelong covenant that involves great sacrifice. Sacrifice is costly, but it produces a great reward.

Early in our marriage, I learned a valuable lesson about sacrifice. Within the first year of marriage, our first child was born, and I enrolled in medical school. I also worked as an embalmer to help provide financial resources for the family. Our finances were often drained because my wife would secretly go buy clothes and hide them in the closet. Some months later, she would wear the item, and I would observe and comment that it was something new. Her response would invariably be, "This? I've had this for a while now." Indeed, she did have it for a while, but it was something she obtained intentionally without my knowledge. She knew that as tight as our finances were, if she had subjected that desire to me, there was a good possibility that I would ask her to defer that desire. In her mind, a deferral was a denial, and a denial was a rejection. My continual requests for deferral were erroneously perceived as me rejecting my wife. In fact, I wanted nothing more than to be the one who provided these things for her, but I did not want to break the bank in so doing.

This rat race went on for several years as we found ourselves digging deeper into debt, with almost $20,000 on credit cards. Of course, the debt was not all from her spending, but her secret spending was not helpful toward our financial cause or the cause of our relationship. When desires of the wife are not subjected to the husband, it plants a seed of discord in the relationship. When those desires are continually rejected by the husband, seeds of disharmony are similarly sown in the marriage. When Darice came to understand that I genuinely wanted to provide these things for her and that her subversion of that process robbed me of the opportunity, things changed. When I understood that my repeated denials were perceived as repeated rejections, things changed. But it required an acceptance, mostly on my part since I am the head, that we are either going to financially thrive or suffer, but we're going to do it together. The vows we took – for richer or for poorer – became real!

Sacrifice is costly, but it produces a great reward.

God gradually began to show me just how much I needed to commit to sacrifice. The practice of sacrifice is not easily acquired. It is gradually learned. For me, it started with buying an expensive cut of meat at the grocery store. I couldn't believe that we were spending $5.99 per pound on a steak – back then that was a lot. We could easily have gotten ground beef for $1.29 per pound or chicken breast – boneless! – for $0.89 per pound. Why would she want such expensive meat knowing that we are struggling? The lesson hard-learned was that extravagance is not wasteful when it serves a purpose more meaningful than its common use. The common purpose of the food was to provide nourishment for our bodies. Consequently, in my mind chicken or the less expensive ground beef was sufficient. But the steak served a purpose much greater than providing nourishment. The steak dinner was a celebration of us. Although we struggled to make ends meet, and there was no likely end in near sight, we still were together. And for at least a moment, we could celebrate and prioritize our time together. Were there ways other than consuming an expensive steak whereby this could be accomplished? Certainly! But this was the most meaningful way for her at that moment. What was, in hindsight, a relatively minor sacrifice was incredibly meaningful to her. However, in the midst of the sacrifice, it was gargantuan because of the severity of our then-current state.

The other lesson that I learned in this exchange is that women, at least my woman, was not built to sacrifice like a man is. The Bible refers to the woman as the weaker vessel:

"Likewise, husbands, live with your wives in an understanding way, showing honor to the woman as the weaker vessel, since they are heirs with you of the grace of life, so that your prayers may not be hindered" (I Pet. 3:7).

It is paramount that we know our wives. The King James Version says to dwell with them according to knowledge. When you spend time getting to know your wife, you will learn to understand how she processes information and perceives circumstances. I am not advocating that you presume to know what she is thinking because that is a near impossibility, especially with women. However, when you venture to understand what she feels and why she feels that way, you start to deal and live with her in an understanding way. You will learn that what you view as a light load or burden may be unbearable for her. I can defer material gratification for years or decades, but Darice just doesn't have that kind of stamina. The desire for external things drives her more than it drives me. However, I am motivated by a desire to please her. This dynamic produces a healthy balance between submission and sacrifice. Sacrifice is proof of love, and submission is evidence of trust. When she trusts that I desire to please and not abuse her, it is safe for her desires to be submitted to me. That confidence does not easily come; rather, it is cultivated by the ardent practice of sacrifice.

Extravagance is not wasteful when it serves a purpose more meaningful than its common use.

When I was in medical school, God plainly instructed me how I am supposed to be willing to sacrifice for my wife. He told me that I could have spent six years in undergraduate college, eight years in medical school obtaining both doctorates, and five years working 120 hours per week in residency training. However, if my wife required me to walk away from my career, I must be willing to do it. That was a commitment not easily made. I had already sacrificed my credit score with credit card bills and expensive meats she wanted to eat. Just when I was on the verge of reaping benefits of my hard work and sacrifice in training, God was now telling me I might have to give it up? He assured me that if I willingly made the sacrifice, I would also be the beneficiary of the sacrifice. I continuously questioned, "So, I become the beneficiary because by my sacrifice, I create for myself, the wife of my dreams?" I wasn't quite buying that one! Nonetheless, I figured, "He's God – I suspect He knows what He's talking about." So, I thought I would give it a trial.

Sacrifice is proof of love, and submission is evidence of trust.

I told my wife, and she immediately laughed with serious doubt. So did I! But the more I began to profess it to her and publicly to others, the more committed I became to it. I started to realize that if we couldn't live harmoniously together, all the riches in the world were useless. Proverbs 21 makes the point that *"It is better to live in a corner of the housetop than in a house shared with a quarrelsome wife"* (vs. 9, 19). Several interpretations of this scripture characterize the house as a mansion or a very large house. You can have all the riches you'd like, but none of it is worth it if you have to live with a contentious woman – one who at any moment is ready to argue or cause an argument. Don't say "Amen" too quickly, brothers, because the next question is, why is she contentious? A woman who understands that she is loved by her husband as Christ loves the church has nothing to contend with. But when she has to contend with work, the football game, alcohol, other women or "fill in the blank" to earn your affection and attention, she can't help but be contentious.

127

The more I confessed my willingness to sacrifice my career for the love I found in her, the less she felt she had to contend with the other distractions in life. Just as Abraham was willing to sacrifice his promised son, Isaac, in obedience to God, I was and am willing to sacrifice my career. Eventually, my wife was able to see the proof of my love – sacrifice. Abraham was not ultimately required to sacrifice Isaac, and I was not required to sacrifice my job – at least not yet. My committed willingness to sacrifice it was sufficient to prove the love I have for her. Your Isaac might not be your career. It might be something else. Are you willing to sacrifice it? What are you not willing to sacrifice and why? Remember fellas, Jesus laid down His entire life for the church. There were no limits to what He would give to prove His love for us. If we have limits in our marriages, we don't love like Christ loved. When we don't love like Christ loves, we don't inherit what Christ inherited. Instead, we continue a life marred by dwelling with a contentious woman.

BUILD THIS HOUSE

"I'll never go a day without your grace. I couldn't have peace without you. I couldn't live life without you."

"Unless the Lord builds the house, those who build it labor in vain. Unless the Lord watches over the city, the watchman stays awake in vain" (Ps. 127:1).

A good man provides for his family. Obviously, he is instrumental in providing food, clothing and shelter. However, he also provides direction for the family – financial, spiritual, educational and otherwise. This can be a daunting task if he attempts to manage it all on the strength of his own abilities. It goes without saying that not every man is well-equipped to function expertly in each of these areas. I am not making the claim that he should or even could be. Nonetheless, he should have some concern and motivation to see that his family is provided for in each area. His goal should be to ensure that his family doesn't lack in any of these. Even this alone is a burden that can be exhausting. The good news is that the burden doesn't fall on the man. It is a burden that should be placed on God. The scripture tells us that no matter how efficient or skillful we might be in building the house, or the family unit, it is in vain unless the Lord is the foreman who oversees and coordinates its construction. No matter how protective any man might be over his family, unless he invokes the Lord's protection over them, he remains defenseless against people or forces that seek to destroy it.

The foundation of a strong household is a strong marital unit. A husband and a wife who, individually, are in close relationship and communion with God presents the basic building block. Jesus, must be the chief cornerstone of that building. This is why it is important to be prayerful and careful in choosing a mate. While beauty and personality might be important criteria for some, these are insufficient to keep the marriage through richer or poorer and in sickness or in health. The mortar that holds the bricks together must be the love of Jesus which is unfailing in every way. According to 2 Corinthians 6 we should not be unequally yoked with unbelievers. While this scripture broadly refers to

Christians being unduly tied to or in relationship with an unbeliever, it is especially relevant with respect to marriages. A yoke is "a wooden bar or frame by which two draft animals (such as oxen) are joined at the heads or necks for working together" (Merriam-Webster Dictionary). The yoke allows two animals to remain in close proximity to each other while jointly accomplishing a particular task such as plowing a field.

The mere mention of the word yoke will conjure up several notions. Yoke invokes unfavorable connotations like subservience, toiling and oppression. These are ripe for discussion in the context of marriage. First, we must understand the purpose of the yoke. Before the invention of heavy farming equipment, a farmer would use draft animals to plow the field for planting crops. A draft animal was one that was capable of pulling heavy loads. While many more animals were capable of pulling the lighter loads, only the draft animals like oxen were used to do the heavy-duty work. In fact, some of the work was too burdensome for one draft animal, so two animals were required.

It was important to optimally utilize the farmland to produce maximum crop. To accomplish this the farmer would ensure that the rows plowed were very straight. If the two draft animals were not harnessed together, they might tend to gradually drift in different directions. A yoke allows the animals to continue along a singular path without straying apart. Moreover, the yoke allows the load to be evenly distributed between both oxen. As the animals proceed along their course, it is the responsibility of the farmer to guide them in such a way that the path they plow is straight. The oxen need only make sure that they are steadily plowing ahead, in step with each other – not drifting apart from or moving ahead of the other. Oxen were ideal for this type of work because they had a slow steady pace and would not thrust their weight with each step to jerk the load like horses or mules did. Instead, the oxen a had smooth, low-gear approach which allowed the farmer to expertly plow the ground.

Obviously, this book isn't about farming, but the analogy of the oxen and the yoke is very appropriate for marriage. With a divorce rate greater than fifty percent, people often think of words like toiling and oppression when they think of marriage. God forbid that the word subservience ever be used in this context. This perspective, I believe is what causes many marriages to fail. They are not built by the Lord or upon His precepts and instructions. There is often a destination that a couple has identified as a goal, but the path is not clearly or evenly plowed due to lack of a sufficient yoke – or an unequal yoke. To provide a visual, imagine attempting to yoke an ox with a horse. Aside from the challenges produced by the incompatibility of their stature, consider differences in their capacity and in their methods.

132

Though the horse might have a more majestic beauty, it is incapable of bearing the load that the ox can. You could theoretically engineer a yoke that binds the two together, but they still will not work in concert to accomplish the goal. The ox will probably bear the bulk of the load while the horse is jerking along its course. The farmer than is less productive in his efforts.

In contrast, when two oxen are yoked together, the farmer can easily guide the path and accomplish the goal. Jesus needs to be the farmer who plows the path for your marital relationship. When you are equally yoked, the path might be burdensome or challenging at times, but an equally yoked partner makes the burden light. Marriage becomes burdensome when you are unyoked and drifting in different directions. Jesus encouraged his disciples, *"Take my yoke upon you, and learn from me.... For my yoke is easy, and my burden is light"* (Matt. 11:28-30).

Subservience has become a bad word in relationship to marriage. Previously, we discussed how difficult it is for men to submit to the authority of another; it is similarly difficult for women. I believe it is more of a challenge for women today than it was in past generations. This is at least in part because subservience is less culturally necessary and is even more unacceptable today than it was in the past. Before women entered the workplace and became more self-sufficient, submission to the male leadership in the home was a necessity for survival. They depended on the income earned by men as the primary source. Women infrequently entered the workplace in a substantial way. When they did, it was often performing domestic work which would earn substantially less money than a man typically did.

Sadly, today the gender gap in compensation still exists. Although the gender pay gap is certainly worthy of note and discussion, it is a different topic for a different book. It is likely that in the past (and present), men wrongly abused their authority, recognizing that there were few alternatives for the woman. Now that women are liberated and independent of a man for their basic necessities – and in many cases have greater financial capacity than a man – it may be difficult to consider resuming a position of subservience again. What I am about to write might seem a bit controversial and too large a pill to swallow, but allow me to fully convey this biblical perspective before you arrive at a judgment.

Marriage becomes burdensome when you are unyoked and drifting in different directions.

God created men to be head of their household. Paul makes this clear in his letter to the church at Corinth: *"But I want you to understand that the head of every man is Christ, the head of a wife is her husband, and the head of Christ is God"* (I Cor. 11:3). We see in this passage, each person including Christ, is subject or subservient to another being. Christ is subservient to God. The man is subservient to Christ, and the woman is subservient to her husband. This is the godly order of the family. The question then arises, "What does it mean to be subservient, and under what circumstances am I to be subservient?"

Before answering these questions, let's first consider the motive or impetus that compels one to be subservient to the other. Why is Christ confident and secure in His submission to God? Christ knows that God's love for Him is infinite. This love will never hurt or abuse Him. Christ has intimate and daily relationship with God. He understands God's thoughts and His motives. Together, along with a probably infinite number of reasons, Christ is able and willing to submit to God.

Now, *when a man worships*, he has daily and intimate relationship with Christ. He understands Christ's thoughts and motives. He knows that Christ will never fail him. He is confident that Christ gave His life as a sacrifice to demonstrate His love for him. He knows that when he calls on Christ, He will answer. The man knows that Christ will never condemn or forsake him. Consequently, the man can be confident and comfortable with his subservience to Christ.

When the relationship between a man and his wife reflects that love between God and Christ or between Christ and His church, there should reasonably be no hesitation in a wife submitting to her husband. In fact, there should similarly be no hesitation in the man submitting to his wife. In Ephesians 5, before he gives instructions for godly order in the household, Paul explains how we should address each other as believers. He tells us that we should submit to one another out of reverence for Christ (vs. 21). In this manner, men should submit to their wives and wives should submit to their husbands.

In marriage, we sadly misunderstand what submission really is. In fact, as the body of Christ who are supposed to submit one to another (Eph. 5:21), we must have a clear understanding of what submission is and how we do it. As previously mentioned, submission is the willful and fervent commitment to the success of a plan or an ideal that you initially opposed. When you submit to a plan or ideal, your former thoughts, expectations and position on the matter are irrelevant. With your spouse, you now have one thought and one goal – that is to make the plan work.

Submission should not be confused with acquiescence. Acquiescence is simply a surrender, after a long-fought battle. It does not imply a commitment to the success of the plan or ideal. In fact, it often permits an unconscious (or even conscious) maneuvering to ensure the failure of the plan. When the plan fails, acquiescence affords the one who opposed the plan the opportunity to smugly say, "I told you so." This is not God's vision of submission. God honors agreement, especially when it is between a husband and wife. If you have agreement, even a bad plan can be successful simply because there was agreement. Imagine Jehosophat's proposition to put the Levites on the front line so they can sing praises and dance before God as they entered into battle with their enemies. Certainly, any army general would view this as the most unlikely of plans for success. But when there's agreement and obedience to God, the forces of opposition are rendered useless, and we become impenetrable to their tactics. Submission and agreement can produce success even from the worst of plans.

I had just completed my residency training, and our family moved to Nashville, TN. I was finally about to start making a decent salary after years of toiling. I had plans to lay some financial foundations to avoid being over-burdened with debt. My initial plan was to rent for a year until we learned the city better and determined where we would best like to live. Well, that plan was sort of implemented because it would be about nine months before they broke ground on building our house and over a year before they finished. During the months of construction, my wife envisioned how she would like to furnish the house. I was concerned because I never had a mortgage payment so high, and it would definitely cost a lot of money to furnish the whole house. Besides, we already had a mountain of debt, including student loans. So, I suggested that we gradually furnish the house one room at a time. In my mind, we didn't need to have a couch or sofa because we could temporarily use bean bags while we furnished some other rooms. Yes, I actually suggested that and was serious! My wife, however, wasn't feeling that idea in the least. I presented my best arguments in favor of my plan, and she still was not persuaded.

Submission and agreement can produce success even from the worst of plans.

After I exhausted every alternative, the Lord showed me the value of the furniture to her. It was not the value I presumed. My valuation was measured in dollars and cents. Her valuation of it was measured in the peace and stability the furniture would seem to provide. I still thought my way was financially the better option, but I submitted. We then went shopping for furniture. I became as much, if not more, committed and excited about furnishing the whole house than she did. In the end, I think I might have offered even more than she required. It definitely was more than what I originally wanted to spend. But that's what submission is. When we decided to move forward, our effort was not marred by me pouting while begrudgingly accompanying my wife at the furniture stores. But rather, my commitment was such that she would never have known that I was initially not on board with this plan.

When we submit to each other, we come into full agreement. Agreement between a husband and wife honors God, and God honors the marriage. When a couple makes a decision to move forward, the yoke is equally placed on both of the husband's and the wife's shoulders. They move in the same forward direction in lock-step with each other. They equally bear the load and most importantly, they don't drift apart. Instead, they follow the steady guidance of the farmer (Jesus) who guides them as they plow the path of their future. In so doing, they lay the foundation for the house – or family unit – they are building. When children are added to this, the husband and wife follow the same instructional leadership of Jesus in the rearing of their children. I could write an entire book focused solely on godly parenting, but a few things are important to note here about how a man who worships parents his children.

Solomon advised his son that *"A good man leaves an inheritance for his children's children,"* (Prov. 13:22). This scripture likely refers to a financial inheritance. However, a legacy of worship is of far greater value than riches. Jesus admonished his disciples:

"Do not lay up for yourselves treasures on earth, where moth and rust destroy and where thieves break in and steal, but lay up for yourselves treasures in heaven... for where your treasure is there your heart will be also" (Matt. 6:19-21).

It is easy to spend an entire lifetime working to accumulate wealth that is passed on to your children after you're gone, but there are much more eternally beneficial things they could inherit from parents. These things will persist for several generations and long after the money is gone. The idiom states, "A fool and his money are soon departed." However, an inheritance of worship is incorruptible.

Abraham was a master worshiper. Everywhere he went, one of the first things (if not the first thing) he did when he arrived was to build an altar whereupon he would offer sacrifice in worship to God. This helped him earn the titles of "The Father of Faith" and a "Friend of

God." Before his covenant with God, Abraham was an idol worshiper. After his covenant, reflected also in a name change from Abram to Abraham, his altar-building endeavors were dedicated solely to God. Each of the four altars Abraham built represented something unique in his covenantal journey with God. The first altar was an Altar of Promise.

A legacy of worship is of far greater value than riches.

God told Abram to leave his clan and head blindly to a land that He would show him. In exchange for his obedience, God would make him a great nation and give him a great name. Everyone that blessed Abram would be blessed by God. Everyone who dishonored Abram would be cursed by God. So, Abram went as God instructed and took his wife, Sarai, and his brother, Lot, with him. The first place they arrived was a place called Canaan. Canaan was a land that was fertile and rich for inhabitance. The Lord appeared to Abram and promised to give the land to his offspring, despite the fact that the land was still inhabited by the Canaanites. Nonetheless, Abram built an altar there to worship. Like Abram, *when a man worships*, he teaches his children to trust in the promise of God and believe to see the promise fulfilled, despite obstacles that threaten to destroy it.

141

Next Abram *"moved to the hill country on the east of Bethel and pitched his tent, with Bethel on the west and Ai on the east. And there he built an altar to the Lord and called upon the name of the Lord"* (Gen. 12:8). This was an Altar of Decision. To the west of him was Bethel, which when translated, means House of God. To the east of him was a place called Ai (or Hai) which translates to a heap of ruins (Strong's Exhaustive Concordance). He situated himself between two polar opposite destinations. On one hand, he could follow after the will of God and partake of all the benefits of servitude and submission to God. On the other hand, he could choose the other path which led to destruction. A man who worships teaches his children to consult God on every decision in his life, recognizing that a single decision can produce blessings or lead to ruin.

Abram moved from his second location and headed southward through a dry and barren desert. When Abram came to Egypt, he was fearful that because his wife was beautiful, he might be killed so Pharaoh could take his wife. Consequently, he made the mistake of telling the Egyptians that Sarai was his sister and not his wife. When Pharaoh took interest in Sarai, the Lord sent plagues unto Pharaoh and his house. When Pharaoh discovered that he suffered these plagues because Abram lied about Sarai being his sister, he sent them both on their way. Interestingly, Abram turned back onto the path that he had previously taken and went back to the first place where he built the altar in Canaan. There again he called on the Lord (Gen. 13). Sometimes, we make bad decisions along our course, despite the best intentions we have. God is faithful to protect us in these errors and redirect us back to the place of His promise. We should never be ashamed to admit these mistakes and share them with our children in hope that they will learn from them, as we have. Those bad decisions, no matter how awful, should not keep us from returning to the altar of the Lord to worship. Instead, we should readily return to this place of safety and prosperity and teach our children to do the same.

After a period of time dwelling in Canaan, it became necessary for Lot to depart from Abram because the land was becoming over-crowded as both of their families were prospering. After Lot departed, God reaffirmed his promise to Abram and told him to get up and walk through all the land that God was promising him. Once again, he was obedient to God's guidance, *"So Abram moved his tent and came and settled by the oaks of Mamre, which are at Hebron, and there he built an altar to the Lord"* (Gen. 13:18). Mamre means strength or fatness (Strong's Exhaustive Concordance). I call this an Altar of Strength. We need to dwell at this altar in preparation for battles that we will undoubtedly encounter as we follow after God and His purpose for our lives. Abram and his family dwelt at the oaks of

Mamre for many years before they heard that his nephew, Lot's son, was taken captive. His nephew was living in Sodom when it was captured. Abram lead his trained men into battle to recover his family and brought them back. But this only occurred because he had the favor of God and because he had spent considerable time worshiping at the Altar of Strength. Like Abraham, *when a man worships* God, he is empowered to snatch his family from grips of captivity.

The fourth altar Abraham built was an Altar of Sacrifice. After many years of waiting for God's promise of a son, Isaac was born. Some years later, God would ask Abraham to do the ultimate act of obedience. He told him to take his son Isaac, the Promised Seed whom he loved, and present him as a burnt offering to the Lord. The next day, Abraham *"arose early in the morning, saddled his donkey, and took two of his young men with him, and his son Isaac"* (Gen. 22:3). By this time, Isaac had watched his father offer worship to God enough that he knew what was required. He asked his father, *"Behold, the fire and the wood, but where is the lamb for a burnt offering?"* (vs. 7). Isaac obviously knew the key ingredient was missing, yet Abraham simply replied, *"God will provide for himself the lamb for a burnt offering"* (vs. 8).

When they arrived at the place the Lord commanded, Abraham built an altar. On top, he laid the wood as usual and then bound his son and laid him on the altar. It seems barbaric and unfathomable that one who was considered a friend of God would even consider going to this extent. But it speaks to the faith Abraham had, believing that God would provide for Himself a lamb. This type of faith in and knowledge of God only comes by having a history of trusting God and seeing Him move. A chorus of the song, Do It Again, by Elevation Worship rings true -- "You made a way, where there was no way. And I believe, I'll see you do it again." This was the conviction that Abraham had that would allow him to go so far as to raise the dagger above his son in preparation to slaughter him in obedience to the instructions of God.

When a man worships God, he is empowered to snatch his family from grips of captivity.

I have to wonder, what was going through Isaac's mind? He obviously was a little suspicious at first because he noticed that there was no lamb. Every time in the past when he would go worship with his father, there was a lamb. But, still there was a trust that his father heard from and obeyed God. This allowed him to follow without question. The Bible doesn't give any indication that Isaac questioned his father any further after that moment when his father assured him that God would provide a lamb. Even when he stacked the fire wood on the altar, it appears that he still trusted his father and his father's faith in God. It would take a tremendous amount of faith for me to get on top of the altar, knowing the process of sacrifice, and at this very point the lamb was still absent. But Isaac continued to trust his father. Even until the very moment when he was about to be slaughtered, it appears that Isaac's faith and trust in his father's ability to hear from God was sufficient to enlist his cooperation. Needless-to-say, God didn't fail Abraham. His faith in God prevailed.

Faith or lack of faith is directly inheritable for our children. Children learn to trust or question God based on the faith or fear they see exemplified in their parents. This is particularly the case for fathers. Consider this. According to LifeWay Research Group, Father's Day has the single lowest average church attendance. Attendance on Father's Day is even statistically lower than Labor Day, Memorial Day and the Fourth of July. In contrast, Mother's Day has the third highest church service attendance, after Easter and Christmas. Why is the day set aside to celebrate fathers so loosely associated with religious or spiritual activities? It is that children aren't interested in or receptive to spiritual instruction from their fathers? Do men not carry a mantle of spiritual leadership? If not, why?

**Data collected by Promise Keepers and Baptist Press show that if a father does not attend church, only about 2% of the time will their children become regular worshipers, even if the mother regularly attends. If the father irregularly attends church, between half and two-thirds of their children will attend church with some regularity as adults. More impressively, another study showed that if the man is the first person in the household to get saved, there is a 93% probability that everyone else in the household will get saved. This staggeringly exceeds the 17% probability of everyone else in the household getting saved, if the mother is the first. [1]

The statistics don't lie. There is a special authority that God has given to men to be priests of their households. It is imperative that men be active leaders of worship – in obedience and submission to God – in their households. Your family is waiting for you to rise up and be the lead worshiper God created you to be. They will observe and learn to trust and submit to God, just as Isaac learned from Abraham.

As men, we usually have very good intentions to be leaders in our homes. We want to ensure that our children are reared to be productive members of society. In many cases, we attempt to do this without consulting

---

[1] Huag, W. and Warner, P, (2000, January). The demographic characteristics of the linguistic and religious groups in Switzerland. *The Demographic Characteristics of National Minorities in Certain European States, Population Studies No. 31, Volume 2.*

an instruction manual or even knowing that one exists. We are left to employ the devices we observed from our fathers, if they were even present. Otherwise, we wing it. God has a purpose for our, our wives' and our children's lives. This purpose is far too valuable to be potentially compromised by us "winging" it. The best instruction manual for how to see those purposes fulfilled is found in the written word of God. He also reveals His personal guidance through His spoken word. However, we have to have relationship sufficient to allow us close enough proximity to hear His voice. Without hearing His instructive guidance, our efforts – no matter how honorable – are futile.

TAKE MY LIFE

"I'm giving my life to you – everything I've been through, heartache and the pain, sunshine and rain. Leaving my past behind me – reaching for a brighter day, believing your plans for me are good."

"An altar of earth you shall make for me and sacrifice on it your burnt offerings and your peace offerings... In every place where I cause my name to be remembered I will come to you and bless you"
(Exod. 20:24-25).

When Moses lead the children of Israel out of Egyptian captivity, they settled in the wilderness of Sinai. God understood that the people needed instruction on how to remain in His favor. He promised that if they would obey His voice and keep His covenant, they would remain His treasured possession among all people of the earth. They would be a kingdom of priests and a holy nation. It is curious that God desired for them to be a kingdom of priests. Prior to this time, there had not been a mention of an order of priests or a priesthood. In fact, there were few mentions of priests before this time. Melchizedek was a priest of the Most High God who blessed Abraham after he defeated Chedorlaomer and other kings who held his nephew captive (Gen. 14:18). Jethro, Moses' father-in-law, was a priest as well (Gen. 3:1). However, there had never before been a "nation" of priests. But this is what God desired his people to be unto him.

Webster's Dictionary defines a priest as one authorized to perform the sacred rites of a religion, especially a mediator between man and God. In the Old Testament, priests were the leaders of society because they were that mediator between God and man. They would hear from God and convey the information to the children of Israel. As mentioned, there were relatively few, but after their deliverance from captivity, God desired to make the entire nation, a kingdom of priests. Before this nation of priests could be established, they needed commandments from God, which they would obey as a prerequisite to their calling.

In the twentieth chapter of Exodus, we learn that God gave Moses ten commandments which they were instructed to follow. These commandments came before He instituted His laws for worship. Because obedience is the element of worship that allows us to commune again with God, the people needed a law to obey before they could worship. Without the law, the people could not readily know when they were disobedient and consequently outside of God's will. In that case, they would have no accountability. With the law, however, they could be assured that they were compliant with His will and thereby remain in favor and communion with God. After receiving the ten commandments, Moses was given detailed instructions on how the people were to worship.

Worship was intended to atone for sins and to restore right standing with God. There were multiple types of offerings. The Burnt Offering was a payment for sins in general. It showed a person's devotion to God. The Sin Offering was made to make payment for unintentional sins of uncleanness, neglect or thoughtlessness. It restored the sinner to fellowship with God and showed the seriousness of sin. The Guilt Offering was given to make payments for sins against God and others. With the Guilt Offering, a sacrifice was made to God, and the injured person was repaid or compensated. I'll diverge to make a singular point here.

If we transgress our brothers and repent to God but not our brothers, our worship is hindered. Jesus reminds us that:

"if you are offering your gift at the altar and there remember that your brother has something against you, leave your gift there before the altar and go. First be reconciled to your brother, and then come and offer your gift" (Matt. 5:23-24).

It is important to make sure that the relationship with God is intact but also that the relationship between our brothers and sisters remains intact, especially amongst those who consider themselves followers of Christ.

For the children of Israel, the three aforementioned offerings were mandatory. They required the offering of a sheep or goat, a bull and a ram, respectively. Each animal had to be without blemish if it were to be offered as a recompense for the people's transgressions. While there were other offerings such as the Offering of Well-Being and the Grain Offering, these were voluntary and were used to express gratitude to God, to show honor and respect to God or to symbolize peace and fellowship with God. But, when an offering to atone for sins was offered, it required the sacrifice of a specific animal. The worshiper must place his hands on the head of the animal prior to it being given to the priest. This symbolized the transference of sin from the worshiper to the animal, which had no sin or blemish. After the animal symbolically took on the sin of the person(s) who offered it, the animal was then sacrificed to God to atone for the sins. That animal would then be sacrificed and burned on the altar.

> *"An altar of earth thou shalt make unto me, and shalt sacrifice there-on thy burnt offerings, and thy peace offerings, thy sheep, and thine oxen: in all places where I record my name I will come unto thee, and I will bless thee. If thou wilt make me an altar of stone, thou shalt not build it of hewn stone: for if thou lift up thy tool upon it, thou hast polluted it. Neither shalt thou go up by steps unto mine altar, that thy nakedness be not discovered thereon."* (*Exod. 20:24-26, KJV*).

It is worth noting that when God gave the instructions to build the altar, He wanted to make sure it was made of earth. Earth was His preference because it lessened the likelihood that the altar itself would become an idol. If it were made of stones, it could be formed into an ornate structure or one that resembled man or an animal which increased the likelihood of idol worship. He gave further instruction that if they were to make the altar of stone, it should not be hewn stone, meaning it shouldn't be carved or shaped using an ax, pick or other structure. If they did such, the altar would be profaned for the same reason.

When God desires worship, He wants it to be free from adulteration by our own imaginations or creations, lest we take pride in it. We sometimes have a way of determining the worship that would be best suited for God and ignore the worship that God himself specifically has requested. Saul did exactly this when he disobeyed God. God told him to destroy all the inhabitants of Amalek; instead, Saul preserved the best of the cattle and the finest of all the spoils with the alleged intention of offering them to God as sacrifices. This is not what God required or requested. He simply wanted obedience. We don't get to modify his commandment to presumably enhance the sacrifice he requested. The audacity to think that we could offer a sacrifice more excellent than the one God himself requests is unbelievable and unacceptable! Obedience is better than sacrifice, as Saul learned (I Sam. 15:22).

When Jesus, who was without blemish, was slaughtered for our sins, the need for the sacrifice of animals on the altar was obviated. However, God still desires altars of earth. He desires that our earthen bodies now be offered as living sacrifices, holy and acceptable unto him which is our reasonable service (Rom. 12). I like the translation of the Life Application Bible, which says that this is our "spiritual worship." You might recall the reference to spiritual worship in John 4: *"God is spirit, and those who worship him must worship in spirit and truth"* (vs. 24). The spiritual part is the surrendering of our bodies as living sacrifices to Him. The truth part is being honest about who and where we are in relationship with God – being honest about our sins and shortcomings and not trying to hide them.

The byproduct of worship that is acceptable and pleasing to God is blessings.

David demonstrates this best in Psalm 51 when he pleads with God, to blot out his transgressions and to wash him from his sin. He readily acknowledged the presence and the severity of his sin – not just that it was against himself or another person, but it was against God and that it was evil in God's sight. Because he had relationship with God, he understood that God delighted in truth on the "inward parts." These things cannot be hidden from God. It is worth reading the entire passage to see David's full and complete acknowledgement of his sin. Therein, we see his commitment to be used in service to God, teaching others to follow him (vs. 13) as well as offering praise to God for the cleansing of his own sins. He concludes his petition with a profound insight: *"For you [God] will not delight in sacrifice, or I would give it, you will not be pleased with a burnt offering. The sacrifices of God are a broken spirit; a broken and contrite heart, O God, you will not despise"* (vs. 16-17).

The sacrifice that God desires is a heart that is genuinely sorrowful and repentant for the sins that have been committed against God. He is much less concerned about all the other accoutrements of worship. He doesn't value the act of sacrificing a lamb or goat. He is not impressed with the act of tearing your clothes as a symbolism of sorrow as many in the Jewish culture of the time did. He is not influenced by the act of charity you performed to appease the guilt you feel from your transgression. In fact, God is not moved by your fabricated tears or lifted hands, if they aren't underwritten by a genuine heart of repentance. Instead, God seeks those who will worship Him in the type of truth that results in a broken spirit and a truly contrite heart. He desires the commitment of those who will surrender their bodies – their wills, desires, plans, motives, etc. – to Him as their spiritual worship. God is looking for those who will acknowledge their sins and take full responsibility for the sin – those who will sorrowfully feel the weight of separation from God that sin produces.

Besides, it is futile to try to hide our sins from God. Psalm 139 tells how God searches our hearts and knows us. Before a word is even on our tongue, God knows it. There is nowhere we can flee from His presence. If we ascend to the heavens or make our bed in hell, He's there desiring to lead and keep us. Only this type of sacrifice is acceptable to God; it is our reasonable service or spiritual worship. When it is holy and acceptable to God, He records His name there. He gives our worship His seal of approval. When that happens, He promised that He will come unto us and bless us. The byproduct of worship that is acceptable and pleasing to God is blessings. The blessing must always remain the byproduct and never become the impetus of our worship.

In His instructions on building the altar, God told Moses that man should not go up to His altar by steps or else his nakedness would be discovered. This nakedness is not the one that implies complete honesty, truth and openness, though God still desires this. Rather, it derives from the Hebrew word "ervah" which means uncleanness and shame (Strong's Exhaustive Concordance). God is a holy God and he not only desires holiness, but he requires it if we are to enter His presence. Before the priests of the Old Testament would enter in the presence of God or before His altar, they had to undergo extensive rituals of purging and purification or else their uncleanness would cause them to be consumed. When the temple was built, the priest would have a rope tied to him along with a bell so that when he went behind the veil into the Holy of Holies – the place where the Spirit of God dwelt – if he died because of uncleanness, others could pull him out without jeopardizing their own lives.

Since Jesus' sacrifice, we no longer need a priest to enter into the Holy of Holies on our behalf. Through the cleansing offered by Jesus' blood, we can now enter into the presence of God ourselves. Hebrews 4 tells us:

> *"For we do not have a high priest who is unable to sympathize with our weaknesses, but one who in every respect has been tempted as we are, yet without sin. Let us then with confidence draw near to the throne of grace, that we may receive mercy and find grace to help in time of need" (vs.15-16).*

The moment when Jesus died on the cross, the veil in the temple was torn, providing access for us all to come before God's presence, as long as we have had the right preparation (Luke 23:45, Matt. 27:51).

God is not moved by your fabricated tears or lifted hands, if they aren't underwritten by a genuine heart of repentance.

Right preparation is an absolute necessity for approaching the throne of God. I'm reminded of Adab and Abihu (Lev. 10), who offered unholy fire to the Lord and were killed as a consequence. King Uzziah attempted to step into a place for which he was not qualified or prepared. When he tried to offer worship, unprepared, he got leprosy and eventually died with it (2 Chron. 26). When David was transporting the Ark of the Covenant, which represented the presence of God's spirit, to the new temple he built, the ark became unsteady and Uzzah reached out to keep it from falling. When he touched the presence of God without appropriate preparation, he was instantly killed (2 Sam. 6:7). Although the veil was torn by Jesus' sacrifice, God's presence was and is still a consuming fire. We must still approach him in a clean and holy state. Only now, that cleanness is accomplished by professing the blood of Jesus as our sacrifice. If we approached God any other way, it is only by His mercy that we are not consumed.

Once, when I was leading worship at a church in Covington, KY I had a unique encounter and more importantly, a valuable lesson about preparedness. We had reached such a sweet place in worship and in my communion with God, I decided I wanted to draw closer. So, I did. Suddenly, I was overcome by a certain heaviness that I had never before or since experienced. I couldn't articulate what happened and was definitely oblivious of why it happened. After worship, I excused myself from the sanctuary and gathered with a group of brothers who proceeded to pray for me. We presumed it was an evil spirit's retaliation for my communion with God. In the midst of praying, God corrected me and suggested that I be thankful I was not consumed by his fire. I had gone to a place in His presence that I was not yet prepared to go. Because of uncleanness in my life, I was susceptible to the same fate as Uzzah, Adab or Abihu. This underscored for me the importance of making sure that we are forthright with God concerning our sins and are quick to obtain forgiveness and turn from them before we enter His presence. As priests, we must be careful to confess our sins and be purged from our iniquities each time we pray and before we attempt to commune with God.

I've mentioned that because of the cleansing power of Jesus' blood, we are now able to come before God's throne as long as we plead and accept the sacrifice Jesus made. Therefore, you might be wondering if there remains a need for a kingdom of priests. The answer is yes. As we discussed, God's presence is still a consuming fire. Although we have access to the throne of grace, we must be prepared to enter His presence or else we might be consumed. Herein is the need for a royal priesthood.

In his second epistle, Peter encourages the disciples that they are "living stones" who are rejected by men but chosen and precious in the sight of God. He explains to them:

"You yourselves like living stones are being built up as a spiritual house, to be a holy priesthood, to offer spiritual sacrifices acceptable to God through Jesus Christ" (I Pet. 2:5).

Again, we see that the sacrifices that God desires are our bodies, our wills, our passions and drives. All of these things surrendered as an altar and a sacrifice made acceptable by Christ who was the cornerstone (vs. 7). He goes further to say,

"But you are a chosen race, a royal priesthood, a holy nation, a people for his own possession, that you may proclaim the excellencies of him who called you out of darkness into his marvelous light" (I Pet. 2:9).

We are indeed, His royal priesthood. What purpose then do we serve when everyone has access to come before God? As you are aware, a priest serves as an intermediary between God and those who cannot approach God by reason of their uncleanness. We still need these royal priests to intercede on their behalf. Because all people have not accepted the salvation offered by Jesus, there are many who are still unable to safely approach the throne of God.

When I lived in Cincinnati, Ohio we would go out on prayer walks. Before we started the walk, we would gather for worship in the sanctuary, and we would also conclude with worship. One Saturday, as we walked the streets, a gentleman joined us and eventually followed us back to the church for our conclusionary worship. As we finished the last song, the gentleman stumbled to the altar and in his inebriated voice said, "I have a request." Instantly, you could feel the tension in the room rise as no one was quite sure what he might request. Then he removed all doubt when he asked to hear the song, "Amazing Grace." I began singing the song and when I got to the end of the first verse, I changed the lyrics. Instead of singing, "was blind but now I see" I started singing different lyrics that confessed various sins. As I sang, I felt almost hypocritical because I hadn't committed those sins. I had my own list of sins – equally displeasing to God – but they were not the ones I confessed while singing. I almost stopped because I felt disingenuous in singing about something I had not experienced. But the Lord urged me to continue. He said these were not my own sins, but that I was interceding on behalf of this man who, in his current state, was unable to offer holy worship. Through this experience, I came to understand just how valuable we are as those who have been consecrated for the service of God as priests.

Those who are on the journey to consecration but have not yet received justification for their sins, still need intercession. This calling is not one for which we should boast, but humbly receive as a mandate to fulfill God's purpose. Like David, *when a man worships*, he is cleansed from his innate iniquity not for self-edification but so that he could teach other transgressors the error of their ways. Through our intercessions, we can help lead them to the way, the truth and the life, Jesus Christ.

God still desires an altar of sacrifice, and He still uses priests to serve as intermediaries for those who are separated from Him. It requires, like with the priests of the Old Testament, that our lives be wholly dedicated to him. It requires that we daily (or even hourly) take inventory of our iniquity – not for condemnation but to permit continual sanctification. We remain humble in knowing that in our own strength, we are unable to build an altar acceptable to God. In fact, if it were constructed by our own handy work, it at the outset would be unacceptable to God. Rather God, knowing our frailties, is faithful to cleanse us from all unrighteousness, when we confess our sins (I John 1:9). By confessing our transgressions and presenting our bodies as living sacrifices, we perform a spiritual worship that is holy and acceptable to God. While all people now have the privilege of offering this type of spiritual worship to God, they are not all yet prepared to do so. Until such a time as they are prepared, God still desires and depends on a nation of priest who will serve as the intermediary between God and a world of lost people who knowingly or unknowingly long for communion with God.

HIGHER GROUND

"I'm pressing on the upward way. New heights I'm gaining every day. Still praying as I'm onward bound. Lord plant my feet on higher ground."

"Brethren, I count not myself to have apprehended: but this one thing I do, forgetting those things which are behind, and reaching forth unto those things which are before, I press toward the mark for the prize of high calling of God in Christ Jesus"
(Phil. 3:13-14).

Stagnation is an illusion. You're either actively moving forward or passively moving backward. It is impossible for an individual to be lukewarm and remain in relationship with God through worship. Jesus, said such lukewarm people would be spewed out of the mouth of God (Rev. 3:16). It is therefore important that we continue, like Paul did, to press toward the mark for the prize of the high calling of God in Christ Jesus (Phil. 3:14).

In what might seem to be an arrogant proclamation, Paul writes that he would not boast in the flesh even though he, by every earthly standard, had reason to. In an effort to declare the surpassing value of knowing and living for God, Paul states,

"... If anyone else thinks he has reason for confidence in the flesh, I have more: circumcised on the eighth day, of the people of Israel, of the tribe of Benjamin, a Hebrew of Hebrews; as to the law, a Pharisee; as to zeal, a persecutor of the church; as to righteousness under the law, blameless" (Phil. 3:4-6).

In a matter of a few verses, he ran down his entire pedigree. He was born to the right parents; had the finest of educations; followed all of the religious traditions to the point of being blameless and more zealous than any other. Who had more bragging rights than he? Even still, he considered any and every thing he accomplished or earned by birthright as loss in exchange for the surpassing worth of knowing Christ Jesus. He counted them all as rubbish – dung – that he might gain Christ and know Him and the power of His resurrection (Phil. 3:8).

Stagnation is an illusion. You're either actively moving forward or passively moving backward.

Paul had the right perspective. He had a worship perspective. He understood that no matter how many great things he accomplished in his life, these things were worthless in comparison to the privilege of knowing and being in relationship with God. I am thankful that God has allowed me to obtain a medical doctorate as well as a Ph.D. in pharmacology and cell biophysics, but like Paul, I consider these things useless for me if it means they, or something else, keep me apart from the life-giving presence of God. This perspective requires a much higher thought process than that which comes naturally to man. It is by no means unusual for man to boast of his accomplishments. It took me years to refer to myself as Dr. Mark Williams, and I still have great apprehension when I do. Not because I haven't earned it. Clearly, I've spent many years, blood, sweat and tears aspiring to this accomplishment. But rather, because I recognize that first the accomplishment was provided only by the grace and empowerment of Almighty God. Assuming this perspective requires that we take on the mind of Jesus:

"Have this mind among yourselves, which is yours in Christ Jesus, who, though he was in the form of God, did not count equality with God a thing to be grasped, but emptied himself, by taking the form of a servant, being born in the likeness of men" (Phil. 2:5-7).

Jesus could easily have boasted of His royal deity, but instead humbled Himself to take on the form of sinful man. This is the perspective that worship allows us to obtain. In fact, this is what it means to magnify God. As I previously mentioned, there is nothing that we could say or do that would make God any bigger or powerful than He already is. So, we magnify Him by intentionally making ourselves smaller in comparison. In reality, we are already infinitesimally smaller than He is. But in our own minds and in this earthly realm, we lower ourselves in recognition of and homage to His greatness. This is why people bow before a king or lay prostrate before God. We assume the lowest position possible so that we will not presume to be on a level anywhere near the same as His. In fact, "The lower we esteem our natural posture, the higher our thoughts and spiritual worship ascend".

Jesus spent much of his ministry trying to get his disciples to think a different way – to think God's way. His teachings were often challenging and difficult to accept. For example, he reminded the people of the longstanding law that said anyone who murders will be liable to judgment. But Jesus took it further, under the new law, to say everyone who is angry with or insults his brother will be liable to similar judgment. It was easy for the people to condemn a person, who was caught in adultery, to death by stoning. But the new law Jesus taught said that everyone who looks at a woman with lustful intent has already committed adultery with her in his heart (Matt. 5:28). Perhaps most challenging for the people both then and today was the following:

> *"You have heard that it was said, 'An eye for an eye and a tooth for a tooth.' But I say to you, do not resist the one who is evil. But if anyone slaps you on the right cheek, turn to him the other also. And if anyone would sue you and take your tunic, let him have your cloak as well... Love your enemies and pray for those who persecute you..." (Matt. 5:38-40, 44).*

It is one thing to be sued in court and readily pay the penalty, but Jesus was challenging them to give their accuser more than that which they sought in the lawsuit. He's suggesting that if someone slaps your cheek that you give them the opportunity to slap the other side. I don't believe Jesus is advocating that you avail yourself to physical abuse, in His commandment. Being slapped on the cheek is more socially embarrassing and demeaning than it is physically harmful. I believe Jesus is saying if someone humiliates you, don't be so full of pride that you are unwilling to be humiliated again if it is necessary for the sake of Christ. The target of humiliation is dignity and self-respect. I am not advocating that we self-deprecate to the point of low esteem. To the contrary, our esteem should be great. But our worth should be determined by the love that God has for us, not in boasting of our own accomplishments or acumen.

The lower we esteem our natural posture, the higher our thoughts and spiritual worship ascend.

With this perspective, when someone assaults our dignity, they have instead assaulted our deity – God. It is no coincidence that Jesus identified how we are influenced by money and pride as targets for growth. These two things are most difficult for us to let go. Under His new law, Jesus was saying don't just be content and feel justified by upholding the law, go beyond what is required by the law in your deeds and in virtue. To do so, requires that we devalue the things that we currently esteem highest – money and our self-dignity – and instead esteem God and His service in highest regard. In short, Jesus was saying take your thinking and behavior to a higher ground.

Also, in the fifth chapter of Matthew, Jesus gave what we have come to know as the "Beatitudes" (vs. 2-12). He was encouraging us to take control of our perspectives. If we feel like we are poor in spirit, remind ourselves that the kingdom of heaven belongs to us. If we are mourning, be confident that we will be comforted. He admonished us to know that we don't have to be forceful to acquire the things we need on earth but rather in meekness, we will find our inheritance. Each of the attitudes He highlighted as desirable was associated with a blessing. *When a man worships*, he acquires these attitudes along with their associated blessings. It is evident when he worships because his behaviors are modified. Though he might be angry, he does not allow that anger to cause him to sin. He is able to command his body and refrain from the temptations of the flesh. He exemplifies the fruit of the spirit – love, joy, peace, longsuffering, gentleness, goodness, faith, meekness and temperance (Gal. 5:22). When we assume this higher thought stature, we liberate ourselves and the people around us.

God doesn't just have a higher perspective, but He has the entire perspective.

Paul was busy preaching the gospel, as he was ordained to do, when they encountered a woman possessed with a spirit of divination. By her soothsaying, this woman earned her masters a lot of money. She followed Paul and the other disciples for several days, just nagging. What she said was not incorrect, but the spirit that was within her vexed Paul. She would say, *"these men are the servants of the Most High God, which shew unto us the way of salvation."* (Acts 16:17). After Paul finally had enough of it, he commanded the spirit to leave the woman by the power of Jesus Christ. Immediately, the spirit left the woman. Not everyone was excited about her liberation. Her masters realized that they would no longer be able to gain money from her. Angered by this, they captured Paul and Silas and brought them before the rulers. They accused them of teaching customs that were unlawful. Paul and Silas were beaten and thrown into jail as a result.

It is pretty messed up when you can be captured, beaten and thrown in jail for doing the work of Christ – for liberating people who are possessed by demons. Such was the case with Paul and Silas. They had every earthly right in that moment to be frustrated and to respond according to their natural inclinations. It would be understandable if they pouted, complained or even resisted. But instead, their higher mind arose within them,

> *"and at midnight Paul and Silas prayed, and sang praises unto God: and the prisoners heard them. And suddenly there was a great earthquake, so that the foundations of the prison were shaken: and immediately all the doors were opened, and everyone's bands were loosed" (Acts 16:25-26). It is noteworthy that not only did Paul and Silas's shackles loosen but all the other prisoners were also set free. There are a couple observations to be drawn from this passage.*

First, when you have committed to do the Lord's work, prepare to be persecuted. Jesus told his disciples, because they hated and persecuted Him, they will also hate and persecute you (John 15:18-27). He went further to explain the rationale behind it. Perhaps, when you understand the motive, you can respond like Jesus did and say, "Forgive them for they don't know what they're doing." Jesus taught his disciples to adopt a broader or a higher perspective on the persecution they would endure. He said, "they hate you because they hate me." They hate Jesus because they hate God, the One who sent Him.

God's purpose is greater than our persecution.

This revelation relieves the burden off of you. It takes the focus off you being the one who is hated and/or persecuted and directs it to the real focus of their hatred, God. More importantly, the God who avenges his people has this perspective, and His perspective is much better than ours. God explains this when he says, *"For my thoughts are not your thoughts, neither are your ways my ways, declares the Lord. For as the heavens are higher than the earth, so are my ways higher than your ways and my thoughts than your thoughts"* (Isa. 55:8-9).

There are certainly some things that we cannot completely understand. They are beyond our comprehension. But God knows the end from the beginning. He also knows the process in between. Consequently, God doesn't just have a higher perspective, but He has the entire perspective. In His encouragement to His disciples, Jesus explained at least a part of it. He made it clear that if He had not done the things He did or spoken the words He spoke, they would not have been aware of their sins. However, when He did, they became aware of their sins which imputed accountability and consequence for the sins. He said, *"Now, they have no excuse for their sin"* (John 15:22). Because of the work of Christ and now the work of his disciples, those who continue in sin are guilty of their sins. No one wants this type of pronouncement made over them. When it is made, the one who delivers the message becomes the object of the outrage. You've heard the saying, "Don't shoot the messenger." We are merely God's messengers. We don't have the power to condemn or save anyone. We can only share the good news or the rebuke. We do not impute a judgment – God does. Consequently, He is the one to whom the anger is really directed.

It is a natural human response for people to become defensive and even combative when you make them aware of their error. It is not that we try to lord the mistake over their heads; we simply bring it to their attention. In so doing, we have exposed their flaw while exposing ourselves to the wrath of their inward guilt. Rather than respond in like fashion when they lash out at us, it is important that we remember that we are a royal priesthood who respond in the manner that Christ would – what would Jesus do. For a period of time, that was a cute catchy phrase and became even a fashion fad – WWJD. More importantly, it remains an internal check that we should maintain in our daily lives. When we raise our perspective to a higher ground, we see the

175

bigger picture and recognize that the anger they feel should not be taken as a personal assault, even if it is presented that way. It would seem impossible for Paul and Silas who were beat because they exposed and eradicated the demon from this woman to not take it personally. But they raised their perspective to a higher ground. I can imagine Paul encouraging us that God's purpose is greater than our persecution.

The change I produce is not mediated through the ballot box or a picket line; it is accomplished only through the prayers I offer in secret.

The second point I want to explore about Paul and Silas's response is that while they were imprisoned, they didn't complain. Their immediate response was to pray and praise God at midnight. Midnight, in the Bible, is used as a simile for one's lowest moment. It is sometimes thought as the end of the line – it certainly is the end of the previous day. Similarly, it can be viewed as the beginning of a new day depending on your perspective. Nonetheless, their response was to pray and praise. Their maturity helped them obtain God's perspective. It was a perspective that asserts God isn't moved by your protest but by your praise. It seems that now, more than ever before, we feel like we must always raise our voice and protest injustices in our country. It's the righteous thing to do, we think. That myopic view is errantly used to justify our subverting God's methods of effecting change by using worldly or legislative mechanisms.

Injustices have always occurred and will continue to occur. The question is, what do you do about them? With the advent of social media, our voices are much louder and have much farther reach than ever before. Now, Christians sadly feel like they no longer need to pray in silence, in their secret closets. Instead, they make their voices heard by a world who really doesn't want to hear it. I've seen prominent Christian leaders seemingly assert that prayer alone wasn't good enough – that we must get out and vote. Understand what I am saying. I do believe that it is important to vote and to be active in advocacy for moral and just legislation. I also believe it is important for Christians to be seen and heard. But my question is what is the world seeing and what are they hearing when we present ourselves in the public square? Are they seeing that we are confident that the effectual fervent prayers of the righteous that avail much (Jas. 5:16)? Or, are they seeing the contrary, that we are employing worldly mechanisms and tactics to accomplish what we describe as godly objectives. I try to vote in every election, but I do not expect my vote to effect the change that God calls for. I am vigilant to remember that *"the weapons of our warfare are not of the flesh but have divine power to destroy strongholds"* (2

Cor. 10:4). I do that which is required of me, or that which is my civic duty, being a citizen of the United States of America. But the change I produce is not mediated through the ballot box or a picket line; it is accomplished only through the prayers I offer in secret. Prayer still changes things!

If you lose your witness, you are of no value to the kingdom of God.

When Paul and Silas were at one of their most bleak moments, they prayed and praised. This is what their priestly obligation demanded. As previously stated, we are a royal priesthood that should show forth the praises of God who has brought us out of darkness and into His marvelous light (I Pet. 2:9). The Greek word for praise in the context of that scripture is "arete." Translated, it means a virtuous course of thought, feeling and action. The literal translation is "manliness." It is interesting that at the time of this scriptural writing, manliness was equated with virtue and morality. Just think how the times have changed. Today, manliness is considered almost anything but virtuous. In his writing, Peter was saying that we are called out of darkness into God's light that we might show forth His virtue, His courage and excellence. Later in the same chapter, Peter reminds us that it is a gracious thing when we endure unjust suffering because we are performing the work of God:

"For what credit is it if, when you sin and are beaten for it, you endure? But if when you do good and suffer for it you endure, this is a gracious thing in the sight of God" (I Pet. 2:19-20).

This is why we have been called. We suffer for Christ's sake, as he has suffered for ours – without complaint, revolt or protest. We endure persecution with the same virtue and courage that Christ did.

This brings me to the third observation I have about Paul and Silas's response while imprisoned. The Bible says the other prisoners heard them as they prayed and praised. It is imperative that we understand that when we profess to be Christ's ambassadors and God's nation of priests, people are watching and listening to us. They are observing our response to misfortune and are taking note of how we respond to persecution, whether just or unjust. The church in America has not yet begun to see the type of persecution that will eventually challenge our faith. Even now, we are willing to compromise on moral mandates in an effort to protect the 501c3, tax-exempt status of the church institution. God help us when the real persecution begins!

*You'll know you have crucified the
flesh when vultures gnaw at your
bones, and you refuse to retaliate.*

The world and those who are imprisoned by the world's ways are quietly standing by watching and listening. What are they hearing and what are they seeing? Are they seeing the "arete" that we are supposed to show forth? Are they seeing evidence that we have been called out of darkness, or are they seeing behaviors that are not fundamentally different from what would be their response in a similar situation? We are supposed to be a peculiar people. This peculiarity captures the attention of onlookers and should compel them toward righteousness. The Bible instructs us to let our lights shine before others so they may see our good works and give glory to God who is in heaven (Matt. 5:16). However, I am concerned that our message is not attractive. I am not convinced that in this season, we are drawing people to Christ at such a crucial and opportune time.

There is much tumult in the world that presents a prime opportunity for Christians to show forth the good works and good news of God. But the message is being lost because we are too busy playing victim. We cry, "woe is me" because someone prefers that you use the words Happy Holidays instead of Merry Christmas. We get bent out of shape when we receive bad press or even are sued for refusing to sell a wedding cake that has decorations depicting a gay couple. We should expect this type of treatment when we stand up for the gospel – it was promised by Jesus himself. But our response should be much different than it sadly is. Because our reaction so closely mimics the response expected from the world, we are losing effectiveness in our witness. Have you forgotten? *"You are the salt of the earth, but if the salt has lost its taste, how shall its saltiness be restored? It is no longer good for anything except to be thrown out and trampled under people's feet"* (Matt. 5:13). If you feel like the world is winning, it's only because you have lost your savor and assumed the position your thoughts and behavior demand – beneath the feet of the world.

Arise, oh nation of priests! Ascend unto the hill of the Lord and offer there a sacrifice unto God upon the altar of earth. Render your reputation, your pride, your will and your entire being to Him as a living sacrifice. Assume a position of higher thoughts and perspectives that permit visualization of God's entire plan. Recognize that the persecution you receive is not because of who you are or because of what you believe, but because of who you represent. Understand that the antagonism of those who despise you and your walk with God are motivated by the agony inflicted by the exposure of the world's sin. Submit to the persecution and endure it even as Christ endured the cross, knowing that the world is watching your response to determine if you really will show forth the courage, virtue and excellence that being Christ's royal priesthood requires.

God isn't moved by your protest but by your praise.

Remain salty, not bitter. Know that if you lose your witness, you are of no value to the kingdom of God and subject yourself to being trampled by the world. We still win, as the ordained nation of priests we have been called. We continue to show forth the praises of Him who has called us out of darkness into his marvelous light. *"Who shall ascend the hill of the Lord? And who shall stand in his holy place? He who has clean hands and a pure heart, who does not lift up his soul to what is false and does not swear deceitfully. He will receive the blessing from the Lord and righteousness from the God of his salvation"* (Ps. 24:3-5).

When a man worships, he crucifies his flesh and is thereby able to ascend into the high place of the Lord. From that vantage point, he does not allow the taunting or attacks of the world to sway his stance. You'll know you have crucified the flesh when vultures gnaw at your bones, and you refuse to retaliate, because the flesh is dead. They can have this carcass (figuratively, of course) and devour it however they choose. Your sight is to remain on much higher ground.

WRAPPED UP

"Always on my mind, and you're with me all the time. Your love entices me."

"You keep him in perfect peace whose mind is stayed on you, because he trusts in you" (Isa. 26:3).

We should think about what really captivates our mind and attention? What entices us? David said, "as the deer pants for flowing streams [of water], so pants my soul for you, O God. My soul thirsts for God, for the living God. When shall I come and appear before God?" (Ps. 42:1-2). How often have we longed for God like this?

It is a sad commentary that most of us can think back to some point in our lives when we longed for the intimate company of a romantic interest. We call it being in love. We awaken in the morning, and this person occupies the first thoughts of our day. At night, it seems we can't go to sleep for longing to spend a few more waking hours with our amore. Maybe a couple times throughout the day, we pause to send a text just to remind her that we are thinking about her. This is the kind of love David apparently had for God. Rarely can we describe our love and pursuit of God with this type of passion. How impactful would it be if we desperately longed for the companionship of God? I'm not sure this is the scripture it came from or if it even has a scriptural origin (likely not), but I suppose this is what kids today would call being "thirsty" – wantingly seeking the companionship of another.

Jesus said, "If anyone thirsts, let him come to me and drink" (John 7:37). What does that mean? I'm certain He wasn't speaking of a literal thirst. Rather, He was saying if you have a longing for something that you know is missing in your life, come to Him and He will satisfy the craving. People spend much of their lives thirsting or longing for something that we can't really identify. We try to quench that thirst with a variety of "beverages." Some are literally beverages (alcohol, for example), while others are figurative beverages. We try to satiate the longing with food, sex, drugs, sports, work, pornography or any number of substitutes only to find that they are not completely gratifying. So, we foolishly try to heap onto the problem even larger quantities of the same substitutes. Eventually, we realize that nothing we've tried has been able to completely satisfy the cravings of our soul. Then, Jesus comes along our path with an offer we try to, but really can't refuse.

Jesus was intentionally on His journey to Galilee and made a pitstop in Samaria. The Bible doesn't say it, but I'm convinced he knew there was a woman there who was "thirsty." While in Samaria, Jesus stopped at Jacob's well and sat at the side of the well. The Bible said that He was weary from His journey, but it didn't state how long He sat beside the well waiting for this woman to appear. Strangely, He did not draw from the well Himself despite the presumption that He was thirsty. Perhaps it was because He didn't have a vessel with which He could draw the water. Maybe he knew He was destined to have a divine encounter with a thirsty woman and wanted to challenge her to draw from His well.

We think that our encounters with God are happenstance but in reality, God knows exactly where we will be geographically, spiritually and emotionally when it is time for our thirst to be quenched. Such was the case for this woman. When she approached the well to draw water, Jesus said to her, "Give me a drink" (John 4:7). Jesus' disciples had already gone away into the city to buy food. I think if the disciples had been present, they would simply have been a distraction for the encounter God intended for this woman to have. The disciples likely would have rushed to fulfill Jesus' request, blocking the woman from drawing her refreshment.

There are many distractions that keep us from drawing water from the well that quenches all of our thirsts. What is standing in the way of you drawing close to Jesus? What are the competing interests that you have? Men should have the ones leading the chase after God but would rather abdicate the responsibility to women. Women will be responsible for taking the children to church and teaching them the ways of Christ. Just as the disciples might have nudged the Samaritan woman out of the way of rendering service to Jesus, we allow other people to step in and offer the sacrifice that God intends for us to render. And, if we had done it, we would have received the blessing. Is it that we don't want or need the blessing? Or is it that we are hindered by other unacknowledged forces in our lives? We must begin to honestly explore what keeps us from offering our sacrifice and service to God and begin to intentionally remove those distractions.

A favorite distraction for men is work. It is perhaps the most seemingly acceptable excuse we have. A man who doesn't work, is worse than an infidel, the Bible says. We love to hide behind this excuse because it's defensible. "I can't go to church on Sunday because I need to rest up so I can go get that paper on Monday," we justify. After all, even God rested on the seventh day. Ironically, it is God who allows us to get wealth (Deut. 8:18). Somehow, our pursuit of wealth has become the distraction for our pursuit of God.

Social media and sports are also huge distractions for us. These things allow us to cultivate commonality and relationship with peers but have no inherent eternal or spiritual value to us. There are so many ways to crowd our day and time that it seems almost impossible to squeeze time in for God. If spending time in communion with and service to God is a priority, we will make time for it. For all my brothers who are apt at creating excuses, I will remind you... time is like money; when you don't have it, you must make it.

Without the distraction of the disciples, the woman had no option but to respond to Jesus. However, she responded with apparent baggage that she had from past experiences. She asked, "How is it that you, a Jew, ask for a drink from me, a woman of Samaria?" At the time, Jews had no dealing with Samaritans, and the woman apparently knew it. Moreover, it appears that she might have had some bitter feelings that were being fed by that past experience. Jesus answered her:

"If you knew the gift of God, and who it is that is saying to you, 'Give me a drink,' you would have asked him, and

189

he would have given you living water"
(vs. 10).

The woman was obviously intrigued by His response. At the very least she was sufficiently dissatisfied with her current condition that she would engage Him further. Being somewhat cautious and not wanting to appear too "thirsty" she observes and remarks that He has nothing to draw with from the deep well. Revealing some likely skepticism, she tests Jesus asking where will He get his water from and if He is greater than their forefather, Jacob, who gave them the well. Then Jesus catches her right where she is and says,

"Everyone who drinks of this water will be thirsty again, but whoever drinks of the water that I will give him will never be thirsty again" (vs. 13-14).

In that moment, he spoke to a longstanding thirst that she had – a craving that had not been fulfilled to that date. Jesus' offer cut through all the excuses and apprehensions she had about opening herself up to the admission that she was thirsty, looking for something she had not yet found. Hoping that her yearning could finally be silenced, she responded, *"Sir, give me this water, so that I will not be thirsty or have to come here to draw water"* (vs. 15).

This woman came to the well broken. Her desire to never come there again to draw water suggested that it was a task of which she was not very fond. Out of necessity, she found herself returning to the same spot in search of something that provided only a temporary remedy for her. Have you ever found yourself doing the same thing over and over, knowing what the outcome was going to be? For some reason, however, you kept repeating the same actions, hoping that somehow the next time the response would be different. It's like being in a bad relationship and having the same fight again and again. You know what initiates it. You know how the fight is going to go down. You also know how it will end. You have gone through the cycle so many times already that you can choreograph the entire dance before the music begins. The only thing you don't know is how to break the cycle.

Our pursuit of wealth has become the distraction for our pursuit of God.

An open encounter with Jesus is the only answer. He is the one who can make it so that you never thirst again or find yourself back in the place you dread. People who struggle with addictions, whether to food, drugs or pornography, can tell you all of their triggers. They know what environments or circumstances will catapult

191

them back into that destructive gerbil wheel that keeps them continuously running but arriving at no place. A Jesus encounter that puts an end to the vicious cycle starts with a holy discontent with your current state.

Discontent for your current condition, creates motivation for change. If you never realize that your current state is beneath the standard God intends for you to live or beneath what you believe it could be, you will never seek a better option. This woman at the well understood that her life lacked a lasting contentment. She obviously has had several failed relationships with men, and the one she was currently with was not her husband. The Bible doesn't explain why the relationships failed, but it does depict the very image of a woman who, by our modern definition, would be considered "thirsty." Her relationship with multiple men would certainly have been frowned upon by other women of her day. This might explain why she came to the well alone and at an unusual time of day, when most women came with a companion at a time when the heat was not so bad. Regardless of the backstory, this woman accepted that she was discontent with her current situation. However, what she did not know was how to remedy the disquiet within her.

Discontent for your current condition,
creates motivation for change.

In her initial encounter with Jesus, she had her guards up. I could picture her rolling her head when Jesus asked her for a drink even saying, "Oh no he didn't just ask me for a pail of water!" God sends people in our lives all the time to bring refreshing to us, but we refuse to accept it because of our presuppositions about who they are and what their motives are.

When I was in undergraduate college, I changed my major to Mortuary Science. I was introduced to a funeral director who I later came to realize was sent by God to be a major help to me. However, I didn't know it initially. Shortly after I started working for him, he was quite vocal about me being his "favorite." Although he was quite comfortable with that designation, I very much disproved of it. I didn't like how it might be exploited to misconstrue my intentions or our relationship. It initially posed a problem for my manager because he presumed that because I was a "favorite," he could not appropriately discipline me and that I would slack in my work without him having any course for reproof.

One evening I figured I'd finally let my boss have it. In a loud shouting match, I insisted that he stops calling me his favorite. After about 20 minutes of boisterous argument, he told me to move out of his building, and I was glad to oblige. In that moment on the phone, I completely committed to it. As soon as we hung up, I asked myself, "Now what are you going to do?" I was in school taking twenty-two credit hours of coursework and had few options for working a job sufficient to pay for an apartment. Within one conversation, I destroyed an opportunity I had where I was living in a nicely furnished, two-bedroom apartment, rent-free from someone who wanted nothing but good for me. Thankfully, it was a short-lived contemplation because my boss called back about ten minutes later laughing at how silly the argument was. I concurred – QUICKLY! The lesson God showed me at that moment is that **you** can be so distracted by the cracks in the vessel that you refuse the refreshment it offers. The fact of the matter is that God uses broken vessels to do his work all the time. We want the blessing to always come from someone who is without blemish or flaw, when we ourselves do not meet that criteria.

This Samaritan woman almost had the same missed opportunity because she seemed to be dissuaded by the cracks in the relationship between the Jews and Samaritans. However, she had no idea that the one who offered was indeed without fault. Fortunately, Jesus didn't relent. That's how Jesus pursues us. He understands our necessity beyond our own understanding or acknowledgement of them. The woman then began to make excuses for why her thirst couldn't be quenched. It's not her fault. It's Jesus' fault. If he had a bucket, she would have been able to draw water for Him, and He would then give her the living water He promised. Stop making excuses for why you can't get off the gerbil wheel. Jesus stands ready to quench your thirst but only when you are ready to drink from his well. Jesus, being determined to set this woman free, explained again what was available to her when she was ready. In that moment, she had to make a decision. Would she continue to make excuses or finally relent to the refreshing drink Jesus offered? Like this woman, we are fortunate that Jesus is persistent in His pursuit of us. He continues to knock at the door of our hearts, hoping that we will open it so he can come in and restore us (Rev. 3:20).

You can be so distracted by the cracks in the vessel that you refuse the refreshment it offers.

As soon as Samaritan woman relented to her discontented state, stopped making excuses, left her skepticism and past experiences behind and was removed from the distractions, Jesus began His work. He revealed all the junk in her life that she desired to keep hidden. More importantly, He showed her that in spite of her past, she could offer worship that was both pleasing to God and liberating for her. With this acknowledgement, she moved forward and told all the townspeople of the good news, and they were saved by her testimony.

What does it mean to have this thirst that seems to always torment us? Why do we continue to long for something that seems to be missing from our lives? I submit to you that the longing is not produced by a physical need, but rather a spiritual need. Man was created to have relationship and constant communion with God. Even though Adam had unfettered access to God, something within him was able to be enticed by a promise of more. He was given access to the entire Garden of Eden and could eat from any fruit therein, except one – the Tree of Knowledge of Good and Evil. Two forces were at work in this interaction. First, the devil spoke to and influenced the woman who in turn, influenced the man. I am not suggesting that the woman is more influenced by the devil than the man, but I am pointing out the huge susceptibility that men have to women.

Seemingly, both of them had an innate urge to gain more than what they had. Importantly, the thing that is forbidden is the thing that seems to tempts us the greatest. It seems to be human nature that draws us insatiably to the thing we cannot have. If you tell a child don't touch the pot, immediately his attention will be drawn to the pot. It doesn't just happen in childhood, but it persists even in adulthood. The minute the doctor tells you because of your diabetes you can't have cake, the thing you start craving most will be the cake when prior to then you hadn't even considered it. It's not the yearning for the "forbidden fruit" that presents the problem. It's the disobedience in obtaining it that is more problematic. That disobedience caused separation from God in the case of Adam and Eve, and also with us today.

Separation from God creates a thirst that can only be quenched with restoration of relationship. The woman at the well, thirsted for relationship. She thought she would find it in multiple men, but it wasn't until she learned about who God was and His desire for relationship with her, that the disquiet within her was silenced. As soon as she recognized that Jesus was prophet, the first question she asked was, "How should we worship?" He responded, *"You worship what you do not know; we worship what we know..."* (John 4:22). Jesus was prophetically telling her the solution to her perpetual thirst was communion with the Father. In John 7, Jesus explained to His disciples that He would be with them only a little while longer. Obviously, while they were with him, they were in essence in the presence of and in relationship with God (John 10:30). He warned them that after He leaves, they would seek Him and would be unable to find Him. They would also be unable to go with Him (John 7:34). He then proceeded to encourage them that if anyone thirsts, he should come to Jesus and drink (vs. 37). Again, He wasn't talking about a literal drink, but instead *"this he said about the Spirit, whom those who believed in him were to receive, for as yet, the Spirit had not been given, because Jesus was not yet glorified"* (John 7:39). Jesus was saying that apart from me – apart from God – man will remain thirsty. However, He promised that the thirst would be quenched by the Holy Spirit which would come only after He ascended back into heaven to be with God.

At the conclusion of his earthly ministry, Jesus found himself thirsty. While he hung on the cross, Jesus cried, "I thirst" (John 19:28). It is tempting to believe that Jesus' body was thirsty from dehydration. As a physician, it is especially convenient for me to consider this as a motive for His declaration. After all, he had not eaten or drunk anything since before the Last Supper. He then went into the Garden of Gethsemane to pray before he was destined to be delivered to Pilate. He prayed so profusely, that sweat poured from His body as blood would from a fresh deep wound (Luke 22:44). He was then beaten to the point of being unrecognizable. The torn protective barrier of skin likely caused an immeasurable amount of insensible fluid loss, much like that which occurs with severe burn victims. Finally, he had to carry the cross to Calvary's hill. All of these likely produced a medical state of dehydration. In fact, the severe trauma His body sustained likely made the dehydration worse. In cases of severe trauma, fluid leaves the blood vessels and infiltrate into the injured tissue causing inflammation and depleting the blood of sufficient volume to maintain blood pressure. In this state, Jesus was almost certainly clinically dehydrated. He could easily have complained about being hungry. He could easily have moaned about the many stripes He took on his back. He could have railed that He had a splitting headache from the crown of thorns on His head or perhaps shoulder pain from bearing the cross. He could have cursed those who spat upon and mocked him. More so, He could legitimately have complained about the stakes driven through his hands and feet. Of all the things Jesus could have said while hanging on the cross, He said, "I thirst."

If His exclamation was about a physical need, He certainly had more imminent concerns than a parched mouth. Instead, His cry was a lamentation caused by His separation from God. For the first time in His earthly and eternal existence, Jesus was separated from God. Because He bore the weight of sins from the past, present and future world, God was unable to look at Him and departed. This is why Jesus cried out, *"My God, My God, why have you forsaken me?"* (Matt. 27:46). Having been in constant communion with the Father since before the foundation of the world, Jesus finally knew the agony of separation from the living God, and it was more torturous than the stripes He bore for our sins.

We don't fully understand how significantly we are impacted by being apart from God. However, it is revealed in our constant quest for something to substitute for the living water. *When a man worships*, he doesn't allow the distractions of life to interfere with him drawing water from the everlasting fountain. He is able to identify the past experiences and excuses that impedes his path to the well of living water. These obstacles are intentionally eradicated from his life as soon as they are identified. He also understands how these obstacles can be as soft and tempting as the allure of a woman, but can have the devastating effect of keeping him separated from God. Although Jesus has ascended to heaven and now sits at the right hand of God, we have been given a comforter in the person of the Holy Spirit which now allows our thirst to be quenched while we exist on earth. Through the Holy Spirit, we have restored communion with God when we worship. Through worship, we know the beauty of relationship without the agony of separation.

MY LIFE, MY LOVE, MY FRIEND

"My life – everything that's anything to me. My love – every part of who I am and all I hope to be. My friend – I make this solemn vow on bended knee to you my life, my love, my friend."

"Make Me a Sanctuary that I might dwell among them. He communed with them at the mercy seat"
(Exod. 25:8, 22).

By now, it should be evident that worship involves giving ourselves completely over to the lordship of Christ. We withhold nothing from the One who has withheld nothing from us. We are able to stand before the King of Kings and the Lord of Hosts hiding nothing from Him and being unashamed of who we are and all we have to offer. I think of the lyrics of the "Little Drummer Boy." The song tells the story of the birth of the King. The little drummer boy wanted to bring a gift to the king but realized that everyone else was bringing fine and expensive gifts to lay before the newborn king. Because he was poor, the little boy had no extravagant gift to offer. All he had to give was his gift of playing the drums. Unashamed, he played his drums the best he could for baby Jesus (the King). Mary, the king's mother, nodded in approval of the gift he offered. Why? Because it was all that he had. Although it did not compare in worldly worth to the other wealthy gifts that were offered, it was the best he could offer and therefore was acceptable.

Unlike the little drummer boy, we sometimes choose to hold back a portion in our offering of sacrifice to God. We fail to offer our complete selves to God in surrender. There always seem to be some area where we forbid God from intruding. If you're like me, you have a drawer somewhere in your house wherein you hide all the junk you don't want people to see. When you have a visitor coming with short notice, you rush to straighten up the house and into the junk drawer go all the things you have not yet made time to sift through. Eventually, that draw becomes so stuffed that you dread ever going through it and likely won't until it is overflowing. Hopefully, the shame of the drawer overflowing will prompt us to address these hidden issues, but if we have enough space somewhere else, perhaps we'll just start working on another drawer. Eventually, we will either have to do a dump or become comfortable with all of our junk being on display for anyone who visits our home. The person who becomes comfortable with the option is called a hoarder. They have no problem living amongst and maneuvering through paths of accumulated junk. Even when others identify that there's a problem, they continue to blind themselves to the most evident problem.

Many of us have become emotional or spiritual hoarders. What started out as small items that we desired to keep hidden so no one could judge us or know that we don't have it all together, gradually accumulated. Eventually, it spilled over into other areas of our lives and before we knew it, our accumulated junk had become evident to others. Our lives have become so polluted with bad experiences and unhealthy relationships that we can no longer keep them stuffed in a junk drawer. They have permeated our very existence and now have been placed on display where others can see the problem, even if we cannot. If we could see it, we likely might choose to just maneuver around it. It seems too difficult or costly to deal with the junk in our lives, so we become content with the dysfunction as opposed to doing the hard work of house-cleaning or temple-cleaning. Sometimes, the biggest deterrent to doing this work is knowing where to begin.

Many men have unfortunately grown up in a household where the father was absent. For the group of us who did have a father (or father figure) in the house, many times he inadequately demonstrated what it means to be *a man who worships* – one who obeys and submits his life totally to God. The absence of a father in the life of a man has a significant negative impact on that man's development, whether he acknowledges it or not. Even when we do acknowledge it, we continue to maneuver around its impact, as if it never existed. All the while, God is desiring to make us whole. But he can never do it until we acknowledge that we are harmed in some way by that deficiency.

I was fortunate to have a father who, despite his flaws, was committed to making sure that his family knew the ways of God – the best way he knew how. Each Sunday morning, he would bring us to Sunday School and to church where we would be taught God's precepts. He died in a boating accident when I was nineteen years old – just as I was learning what it meant to be a man and specifically how to navigate being a Black man in our society. I never had an opportunity to glean from him the tools I needed to maximize manhood. Shortly after my father's death, I was again fortunate to have found a mentor – my former employer, Donald

Jordan, Sr. He not only became a father figure to me privately, but he announced and advertised publicly that I was his son, in whom he was well-pleased. No discredit to my father, but I became his son and learned from him much of what I needed to mature in manhood.

There is something vitally important about a father's affirmation of his son. Jesus, being God manifested in the flesh, was acknowledged publicly by His father. Immediately after He was affirmed, Jesus was led into the wilderness where He would be tempted by the devil. Because God doesn't do things haphazardly, He knew that the affirmation needed to come before Jesus was tempted. The affirmation was key to Jesus being prepared not just for the temptation but also for the work of ministry that He was ordained to do.

One of best gifts I ever received was a piece of wall art from my oldest son. It featured the inscription, "A father is a son's first hero." Boys need a father to mimic or imitate until they are old enough to understand the motive behind the behavior and adopt the underlying principles themselves. The affirmation from the father might not be necessary for success, but it sure gives a man a head start in this race. Young boys and young men need to be encouraged by a male figure that sees the gift God placed in them to help it manifest. As confidence and assurance is developing, it is fragile and will need edification to reach its full maturity. Key verses regarding parenting directly address men: *"Fathers do not provoke your children to anger, but bring them up in the discipline and instruction of the Lord"* (Eph. 6:4). Another scripture admonishes, *"Fathers, provoke not your children to anger, lest they be discouraged"* (Col. 3:21, KJV). Why do you suppose the Bible specifically gives this instruction to fathers and not mothers? Perhaps it is because children are much more disheartened when they do not have the approval of their fathers. Maybe there is a perception (possibly misperception) that a father's approval is a bit more merit-based than a mother's. Momma is going to cheer you on no matter what, but Daddy will light into you if you are slacking, especially a male child.

Paul admonished the Christians in Corinth, *"For though you have countless guides in Christ, you do not have many fathers. For I became your father in Christ Jesus through the gospel"* (I Cor. 4:15). He was saying that true leadership requires more than instruction; it demands an impartation. Better than pointing you in the right direction, I should lead you down the right path. It requires that I have close, open and honest relationship with my brothers in Christ. An important prerequisite for developing a lifestyle of worship, is having it first demonstrated before you. Paul advised the church to become "imitators" of him (vs. 16). He wasn't suggesting that they just mimicked his words or gestures, but rather that they adopt the mind of Christ as he adopted it. He encouraged them to walk in the demonstration of God's power and not just talk about it: *"For the kingdom of God does not consist in talk but in power"* (vs. 20). Importantly, Paul concludes this chapter with a key question, *"What do you wish? Shall I come to you with a rod, or with love in a spirit of gentleness?"* (vs. 21) Like a father would not withhold chastisement of his son who was wayward, Paul was saying, if I need to, I will come to you with correction. You know what you ought to do and consequently will make the decision to do right or to be held accountable for it.

Because we do not have many fathers (natural or spiritual), men sometimes lack the accountability that only a father can enforce. We are so emboldened by the absence of men who would hold us accountable that we don't care if our "junk" is on full display. Our spiritual and emotional hoarding becomes egregious, and we don't bat an eye at it. How can you possibly have three or four children out of wedlock, refuse to pay child support for them and not have shame for it? How can you brazenly flirt with every pretty skirt that walks past you, especially when you're married? How can you willingly lie about the income you earned under the table and still claim to be one who is a follower of Christ? We do it because we don't have many fathers.

Leadership requires more than instruction; it demands an impartation.

In the church, there is a deficiency of male mentors who are willing to demonstrate what it means to worship. Even among those who are willing to demonstrate submission and obedience to God, few are willing to break out the rod on our brothers who refuse to measure up. We allow them to continue with their hoarding. When we commit to God, we commit to availing every aspect of our lives to Him. Every part of who we are and all we hope to be must be submitted to him. If there are areas where we know we are deficient and we need mentorship, we should seek it and stop denying that it is a deficiency in our lives. If we know that there is an area of strength we possess and see a brother struggling to grow in that area, we shouldn't remain silent and hope that he comes to himself on his own. We interject ourselves (politely) into their lives and impart to him the guidance needed to help them overcome. We commit to making sure that the places we've been and things we've struggled through don't become the swamp that entangles our brother.

Jesus told Peter, *"behold, Satan demanded to have you, that he might sift you like wheat, but I have prayed for you that your faith may not fail. And when you have turned again, strengthen your brothers"* (Luke 22:31). He said this knowing that Peter would eventually deny him and have crippling guilt as a result. Peter had no knowledge of how temptation would capture him and swore that he would never leave Jesus' side. Jesus prophesied that before the rooster crowed, Peter would deny him three times. Indeed, the very thing happened. I could only imagine the condemnation Peter felt after denying Jesus, especially considering how close their relationship had been. Peter was one of the few who saw Jesus transfigured in glory on the mountain. There Peter witnessed the glory of God shine on Jesus as he spoke with Moses and Elijah. Afterward, he heard the voice of God endorsing Jesus as the son in whom God was well-pleased (Matt. 17). Peter was the one who had the true revelation of who Jesus was when others could not answer. For this, Jesus himself affirmed Peter saying he was indeed receiving revelation from God (Matt. 16). How is it possible that this very person who had such close relationship with Jesus could deny him? As I've said many times, we never know what we are capable of doing until the right set of circumstances present themselves and cause us to respond in a way that no one else, including ourselves, would have predicted. But Jesus predicted it and encouraged Peter to not beat himself up about his failure. But instead go strengthen his brother after he was again strengthened himself.

God knows that we will fall. He also knows that if we get back up after the fall, we have the ability to use that experience to strengthen someone else. Proverbs 24:16 tells us that even a righteous many falls many times. So, we should not feel so condemned when it happens that we disqualify ourselves from God's use. After Jesus was crucified, Peter was so distraught by his failure that he abandoned his work in the ministry. He went back to what he was doing before he ever encountered Jesus. He started fishing again. After His resurrection, Jesus came to where Peter was fishing and said the very thing He said when they first met. He asked if they had caught any fish. When they answered "no" Jesus told them to cast the net on the other side of the boat. Immediately their nets were full despite having caught nothing all night. Prior to this miraculous feat, they didn't recognize that the man who called out to them was Jesus resurrected. After the miracle, Peter recognized Jesus, jumped out of the boat and swam to meet him. After they finished eating, Jesus asked Peter, "Do you love me?" Peter responded, "Of course I do." Jesus told him to feed His sheep. Jesus then proceeded to ask the question a second time and Peter responded in the affirmative. Jesus told him again to feed His sheep. The third time Jesus asked Peter if he loved Him Peter's feelings got hurt. I can only imagine that he recalled the three times he denied Jesus. Perhaps he felt as if Jesus was unsure about the sincerity of his love because he had such a huge failure. Likely still wondering why Jesus asked three times, he answered again, *"Lord, you know all things; you know that I love you."* Jesus said, *"Feed my sheep"* (John 21:17).

After this very uncomfortable encounter, Jesus departed, and Peter followed. Following behind the two of them was the disciple who, at the Last Supper, leaned in and secretly asked Jesus who would be the one who betrays him. Peter was likely feeling a little condemned or judged by his presence. No one wants someone who constantly reminds them of their failure to follow closely behind them. We try instead to put those thoughts out of our memory. Peter asked Jesus, "What about this guy?" Jesus advised Peter that what that man does was none of Peter's concern. In this dialogue, Jesus was essentially telling Peter don't let your past failure, no matter how significant you think it was, deter you from doing the work I called you to do. Also, don't let the others use those past failures to dissuade you from pursuit of your mission. This was the moment when Peter was strengthened again, or restored. After this, he could then do as Jesus commanded him to do; go strengthen his brother.

We need more fathers. We need men who are willing to step up to walk with both children who are young in age and adult men who are young in faith. We need these men to demonstrate what it means to completely surrender to God and submit to His ways. Lifestyle demonstration of worship is imperative for men to witness. It reinforces the truth that communion with God really does answer all things and meets all needs. We need fathers in the faith who acknowledge their own failures and who have recovered from them sufficiently to go and strengthen their brothers. The strengthening that the brothers need is not always just a kind word of encouragement, but may also include a rod a correction. We need to avail ourselves to be accountable to and accountable for our brothers. Most importantly, we would best benefit from releasing the things that God clearly wants access to, so He can perform His corrective work.

We haven't mastered worship until we are able to release our finances for God's discretionary use.

Peter knew that he messed up in denying Jesus. When his failure had been presented unavoidably before him and seemed to disqualify the legitimacy of his love, he recalled and acknowledged that God knows everything. Although others might look at his denial and conclude that he didn't really love Jesus, Peter realized that he didn't need to let his mistake define his love. Peter didn't need to remind Jesus that he knew everything; he needed to remind himself that Jesus knew his heart. We need to remind ourselves that Jesus still knows our hearts. He knows if we genuinely love Him or if there are things we love even more. Whether it is pride, reputation, women or money, God knows the prominence that He and these things occupy in our hearts. While God desires that we give him all the things that we are ashamed of, He also wants the things we are proud of. When it is surrendered unto Him, He uses it how He chooses. Undoubtedly, it will be for our eventual good and not our harm. God speaks directly to us about His goal for us: *"For I know the plans I have for you, declares the Lord, plans for welfare and not for evil, to give you a future and a hope"* (Jer. 29:11). But His plans are not enacted until we give it all to Him, including our finances.

Money is an area where men may have difficulty in trusting God. If you have ever had bad credit and repaired it, you know that you never want to go back to that place again. You also know that if you drove a hoopty (an old dilapidated car) and now have a nice ride, you never want to go back to "old unreliable." Anything that threatens to take us back there, we will avoid with a passion. It is ironic how we can live with all the emotional and spiritual junk in our lives, but refuse to be without extravagant amounts of money. I get it! Even the Bible says that money answers all things (Eccles. 10:19). Money offers protection, much like wisdom does

(Eccles. 7:12). It is hard to let money go once you've had it. But God wants that too.

Paul said, *"I have learned in whatever situation I am to be content. I know how to be brought low, and I know how to abound. In any and every circumstance, I have learned the secret of facing plenty and hunger, abundance and need"* (Phil. 4:11-12). *When a man worships*, he learns to submit everything, including his finances to God. If God so chooses, He can have it all. He usually only requires a tenth of it, but the man who worships is willing to give it all to the King. He knows that his disobedience in holding onto it causes separation from God, which creates in him an unquenchable thirst. We haven't mastered worship until we are able to release our finances for God's discretionary use. We sometimes are willing to let it go when we know it's for a "good cause." But when we don't know how it is being spent or if it is being spent for a cause that we might not necessarily deem worthy, we are reluctant. You can masterfully perform all the accoutrements or expressions of worship (e.g., kneeling, hand-raising, bowing, singing, etc.), but if you are too closely held by money, you cannot enter into God's kingdom.

In the eighteenth chapter of Luke, Jesus encounters a rich ruler who asked, "What must I do to inherit eternal life?" The rich man proceeded to proudly brag that he has kept all of the commandments since he was a young child. *"When Jesus heard this, he said to him, 'One thing you still lack. Sell all that you have and distribute to the poor, and you will have treasure in heaven; and come follow me'"* (Luke 18:22). When the man heard this, he became very sad because he was extremely rich and walked away. Worship is costly. As previously discussed, it can cost us our reputations. It almost always costs time, but obedience can also consume our talents and our resources. It is difficult for many Christians to fathom the concept of tithing. What they see is the departure of 10% of their income and often may criticize how the church to whom they gave the tithe uses it. It is important for us to remember that we do not give tithe to the church, per se. We instead give the tithe as unto the Lord and out of obedience – worship. Giving money does not create relationship with God, but the obedience in following His commandment to do this and everything else he commands, provides access to commune with Him.

You might be thinking, "I'll do everything else – give my time, mentor a brother, study my Bible and even treat my wife right – but I refuse to give money to the church." Money is not easy to part with it because it is vital to most aspects of our lives. From enjoying leisure time to provision of food, money is required. It is especially difficult to part with when you don't have much of it. But even those who have an abundance of it often find themselves devising strategies to hold on to it or get even more. Christians are supposed to have money but instead it seems that money has Christians. When Christians prioritize the worldly economy over God's economy of love and compassion, we dampen our witness. Jesus told His disciples,

"Only with difficulty will a rich person enter the kingdom of heaven... it is easier for a camel to go through the eye of a needle than for a rich person to enter into the kingdom of God" (Matt. 19:23-24).

That rich ruler who inquired of Jesus realized that he would rather keep his possessions than to be used by God in following Jesus. I am not asserting that you must give up all your money to be used by God, and I don't believe that was the message Jesus wanted to convey. However, Jesus did want to expose to the rich man where his heart was. He desires to reveal to us what is in our hearts as well: *"For where your treasure is, there your heart will be also"* (Matt. 6:21). The scripture in Matthew 6 continues, *"No one can serve two masters, for either he will hate the one and love the other, or he will be devoted to the one and despise the other. You cannot serve God and money"* (vs. 24).

Withholding any part that we desire to hide or keep from God is counterproductive to worship. It keeps us separate from God. In the book of Acts, we learn of a man named Ananias and his wife Sapphira. At that time, the church was growing but was very unified in beliefs and possessions:

> *"Now the full number of those who believed were of one heart and soul, and no one said that any of the things that belonged to him was his own, but they had everything in common" (Acts 4:32).*

Consequently, there was not a needy person among them and great grace was upon them all. Anyone who owned a house or land would sell it and lay the money at the apostles' feet. This money would be distributed among anyone who had a need, just as Jesus instructed the rich man to do. But Ananias, with his wife's consent, sold their property and held back a portion of the proceeds. He brought only a part of it and laid it at the apostle's feet. Peter discerned that Ananias withheld some for himself and said, *"Why is it that you have contrived this deed in your heart? You have not lied to man but to God"* and immediately, Ananias died and was carried away (Acts 5:4-6). Three hours later, not knowing what had happened to her husband, Sapphira lied about withholding a portion of the money and also fell dead immediately.

Some might argue that they were stricken dead because they lied. It could also be argued that their sin was withholding that which God commanded them to give. In either case, they continued to try to hide it and were subsequently killed because of it. I am not suggesting that God will strike you dead for withholding finances from Him, but when we do, we only hinder ourselves. In Malachi 3:10-11 God tells us to

"Bring the full tithe into the storehouse, that there may be food in my house. And thereby put me to the test, says the Lord of host, if I will not open the windows of heaven for you and pour down for you a blessing until there is no more need. I will rebuke the devourer for you, so that it will not destroy the fruits of your soil, and you vine in the field shall not fail to bear, says the Lord of hosts."

Again, it is not that God desires or needs our money. Instead, He is looking for obedience that is birthed from an unyielding love for Him. God seeks worshipers, those who will do his will no matter the cost. He desires to commune with those who will obey him no matter how great the sacrifice.

When we keep God's commandments, including giving of time talents and treasure, we elevate our status from servant to friend. Jesus told his disciples, *"You are my friends if you do what I command you. No longer do I call you servants, for the servant does not know what his master is doing; but I have called you friends"* (John 15:15). In the previous chapter, Jesus explained that if we love Him, we will keep his commandments. We cannot claim to love God, if we do not follow His instructions. We certainly can't be considered His friend if we remain disobedient. Instead, we simply honor God with our lips, and our hearts remain far from Him. Obedience to God, as it pertains to the handling of our money, then becomes a significant test of where our hearts really are. Do we love God or do we love money more? Will we obey God or become servants to money? Like the principle of sacrificing for our wives, wherein we become the eventual beneficiary, when we sacrifice financially to God and His prescribed purposes, we benefit. As the scripture in Malachi mentions, when we obey God in giving, He pours out blessings for us that we don't have room enough to receive. Conversely, when we withhold the finances for whatever reason we might use to justify, we bring condemnation on ourselves like Ananias and Sapphira.

"Each one must give as he has decided in his heart, not reluctantly or under compulsion, for God loves a cheerful giver" (2 Cor. 9:7). Understand, it is not my intention to compel anyone to give a tenth or any fraction (greater or smaller) of their money to God. That is not my place. I am merely reviewing what the Bible says about giving. He who sows sparingly will reap sparingly. He who sows bountifully will also reap bountifully (vs. 6). The decision is up to the individual worshiper. While giving is not worship itself, it is an act or expression of

219

worship just as kneeling is an expression of our submission to a sovereign God. *When a man worships*, it is evidenced by how he handles his money. That portion of his money that is intended to be sown, he willingly sows. He uses a portion of it to meet the needs of his family, and the wise man who worships takes a portion of his earnings and invests it.

There was a parable that Jesus told of a man who went on a long journey. To each of his servants, he entrusted money. To one he gave five talents. To one he gave two talents, and to another he gave one talent, each according to his ability. The man went away and returned with an expectation. The servant to whom he gave five talents returned with ten. The one to whom he gave two talents caused it to increase in value and brought back four talents. To each of these two, he said well-done good and faithful servant. But the one to whom he gave only one talent buried it and brought it back to him in the same condition as when the master left. The master called this servant wicked and lazy. He had an expectation that the servants would take the money he gave them and cause it to be multiplied. The kingdom expectation is for increase not stagnation or loss. Anyone who sows money into the kingdom of God doesn't lose it, but rather he expects that it would be multiplied. God also expects that we would multiply our funds so substantially that we become the lender and not the borrower (Deut. 15:6). In the parable, the master said to the lazy servant, *"You ought to have invested my money with the bankers, and at my coming I should have received what was my own with interest"* (Matt. 25:27). So, the master took the money from him and gave it to the one who produced ten talents.

When we are obedient to handle money the way God intends for it to be managed, we will not only multiply that money with kingdom returns of blessings but also with interest earned in the marketplace. However, it requires that we do it God's way. We render unto God his portion, unto the government its portion and provide for the needs our family has. A portion of what is left is placed for an inheritance to our children and portion is used to invest in the market place. Proverbs 6:6-8 explains how It is wise to store up provisions for a later time, and the passage in Matthew is evidence that wise investment is consistent with godly principles.

The kingdom expectation is for increase not stagnation or loss.

When a man worships, his love for God causes him to surrender his life to God. This manifests as obedience to God in all aspects of his life. In keeping God's law, he attains a "friend" status with God that permits constant communion with Him. Obedience is not always easy and is often costly. But when it is acceptable to God, it produces a return that blesses us. While there are innumerable impediments to a man assuming this position of worship, when he identifies these distractions, he is able to address them by immersing himself in the word of God. He learns to crucify his flesh by denying his carnal drives the stimuli and expressions they require for survival. He realizes that this is not able to be accomplished without the empowerment of God's grace and the encouragement of fathers in the faith. Consequently, he avails himself to be made new and released from the bondage of his past by renewing his mind. He assumes the mind of Christ which allows him a God's eye view of his situation. From the vantage point of higher ground, he sees how the plan of God is working together for his good. *When a man worships*, his life and his love are completely dedicated to his friend – God.

The Author

Dr. Mark Williams is a native of Cincinnati, Ohio where he attended the University of Cincinnati for his undergraduate studies. At the age of nineteen years, he experienced the tragic death of his father and brother in a boating accident. After this, Mark felt led by God to pursue  training in mortuary science. He transferred his course study to the Cincinnati College of Mortuary Science where he graduated *Suma Cum Laude*. In 1994, one year after marrying his high school sweetheart, he matriculated at the University of Cincinnati College of Medicine while working as a funeral director and embalmer. He became only the second African-American to graduate from the college's Physician Scientist Training Program, where he obtained his Medical Doctorate (M.D.) and his Doctorate of Philosophy (Ph.D.) in Pharmacology and Cell Biophysics. He continued at the University of Cincinnati College of

Medicine and completed his residency training in Otolaryngology – Head & Neck Surgery, prior to relocating to Nashville, Tennessee.

Dr. Mark, as his friends and acquaintances affectionately call him, is the founder of Ear, Nose & Throat Specialists of Nashville and the Voice Care Center of Nashville, where he currently works as a solo practitioner. His desire to help professional and aspiring Gospel/Christian music singers with voice problems was his primary draw to Nashville. He has become known to the Gospel music industry as "The Voice Doc" and frequently conducts seminars and workshops on the care of the voice, as well as the use of the voice in worship.

Mark is the ninth of ten sons born to his parents. They were reared in a Christian household, attending church weekly. At the age of seven years, Mark accepted Christ into his life and has attempted to live the lifestyle of faith ever since. Of course, he's made the usual mistakes along the way, but never lost focus on the necessity of spiritual relationship with God. In undergraduate college he pledged Kappa Alpha Psi Fraternity, Inc. and began his exploration of singing as a Gospel music songwriter and vocal artist. For over 20 years, Dr. Mark has served as a worship leader in several churches. While serving in this capacity, he has extensively studied the biblical basis for and expressions of worship. He is a prolific teacher of this subject matter.

Dr. Mark is also an award-winning recording artist who has two nationally released projects to his credit – "Everything" and "When A Man Worships." The second CD, and his vast experience in the study of worship inspired the writing of this book.

For twenty-seven years, Mark has been married to his wife, Darice. Together they have three children: Demarcus, Aaron and Courtney. All three of their children were born during his lengthy medical school education and residency training. Mark recalls that his highest priority in training was, "to finish with the same wife I started with." Given the demands of his chosen path, coupled with the contemporaneous challenges of parenting, this arguably was a lofty goal. It appears he is well on his way to meeting it, while he continues *merging music, medicine and ministry.*

Follow Dr. Mark Williams on Social Media:

@DrMarkWill

Download the music CD for free:

Visit www.DrMarkWill.com

Or

Made in the USA
Middletown, DE
05 September 2022